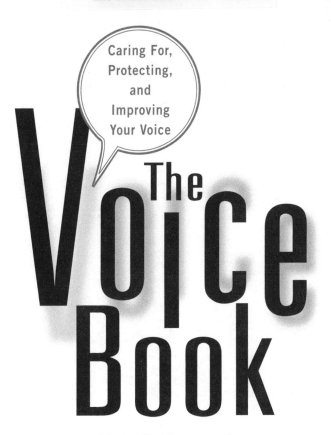

Caring For,
Protecting,
and
Improving
Your Voice

The Voice Book

Kate DeVore and
Starr Cookman

CHICAGO
REVIEW
PRESS

Library of Congress Cataloging-in-Publication Data
DeVore, Kate.
  The voice book : caring for, protecting, and improving your voice / Kate
DeVore and Starr Cookman. — 1st ed.
      p. cm.
  Includes bibliographical references and index.
  ISBN 978-1-55652-829-3
  1. Voice—Care and hygiene. 2. Voice culture. 3. Voice—Physiological
aspects. 4. Speech—Physiological aspects. I. Cookman, Starr. II. Title.

  QP306.D48 2009
  612.7'8—dc22

                                                              2009006436

Cover design: TG Design
Interior design: Jonathan Hahn
Photographs: Starr Cookman
Illustrations: Linda Tenukas

Published by Chicago Review Press, Incorporated
814 North Franklin Street
Chicago, Illinois 60610
ISBN 978-1-55652-829-3
Printed in the United States of America
10 9 8 7

To our many teachers, who take the shape of
professors, clients, family, and friends.

Contents

Acknowledgments

We owe a tremendous debt of gratitude to those teachers from whom we have had the privilege to learn. While much voice training has historically been passed from teacher to student orally, there are those who have shared their wisdom in written form. Arthur Lessac, Kristin Linklater, Patsy Rodenburg, and Cicely Berry in particular have written outstanding books on voice from a theater training perspective, and we acknowledge and appreciate their value and influence. In the field of voice rehabilitation, we would like to acknowledge experts Kittie Verdolini, Daniel Boone, Arnold Aronson, Ray Colton, and Janina Casper. As the exact origins of most voice exercises are impossible to ascertain, we are grateful to the collective consciousness that has informed our work. And to our patients and clients—you are the driving force behind our current quest for knowledge in the field of voice. We are simultaneously humbled and inspired by your courage, and it is an honor and privilege to earn your trust and to assist you in a time of great vulnerability.

We thank our agent Rita Rosenkranz and editors Sue Betz and Devon Freeny for seeing the value in this subject matter and shepherding us through the process of publication. We also offer our thanks to our team of editors, Kylee Fenton, Kalia Kellogg, Kittie Verdolini, Bonnie Raphael, Rocco DalVera, Heidi Adams,

Patricia Kilgarriff, and Cynthia Wolcott, and to Hazel Liebert for completing our initial transcription. Kalia Kellogg, you have graced our book with your beautiful face; thank you so much for sharing your time and talent. Our gratitude to Linda Tenukas for her illustrations, Kristine Teets for checking references, and Tim Brown for help with photography equipment.

Kate says: I offer deep thanks to my mentors Kate Ufema, Kittie Verdolini, Bonnie Raphael, Ingo Titze, Julie Barkmeier, and Joy Gardner. Thanks, too, to the gang from Boston (Pam Harvey, Maria D'Antoni, Marvin Fried, Ann, Sue, Rainbow, Ronnie, and Curious George). I also thank the family of friends whose support has been so valuable over the years: Rick Fiori, Ashley Sovereign, Heidi Adams, Liz Baqir, Helen Mathison, Tiffany Johnson, Amy Wink, Miriam van Mersbergen. And especially Jay "Total" White, my rock, playmate, and comfort. My deep gratitude goes to my first teachers, my parents, Patricia Kilgarriff and Duane T. DeVore, for their intelligence, wisdom, humor, creativity, integrity, curiosity, and unconditional love and support. Dad and Linda, I still miss you. And finally a heartfelt thank-you to Starr Cookman for always modeling and radiating compassion, for taking the wonderful photographs in this book, for your freakishly generous spirit, and for taking one for the team by doing all the formatting! It is a delight to be both little and big sis to you, and I marvel at the synergy created by our collaboration.

Starr says: Without my brilliant voice mentors, I would still be aimlessly seeking answers. So much gratitude to Kittie Verdolini, Ingo Titze, Michael Karnell, Linda Carroll, and Jenny Hoit. For inspiration in the art of voice, many thanks to Onalee Grimes, my first voice teacher, and to my singing and musical guides, Kathy DeJardin, Richard Franz, and Angela Cofer. To my family, Darrell, Rowan, and Ella. Without your patience, love, and help, this book would not have happened. A shout out to Denis

Lafreniere, Patricia Doyle (my yardstick), and Janet Rovalino, fellow members of the University of Connecticut Voice Team, for collaboration and support. Kylee Moreland Fenton, my bestest, thank you for 30 years of the truest friendship I have ever known. You have centered me, inspired me, and supported me tirelessly throughout this process. Mom, Dad, Ann, Bill, and Paul, thank you for your love and support. Gratitude to Michelle Begley for kid-care and music therapy. Last, I would like to acknowledge my coauthor, Kate DeVore. Her knowledge and brilliance extends both deeply within the field of voice care and so far beyond it. She has been a catalyst for me to expand professionally and personally, breaking molds I didn't even know I had placed on myself. Kate, thank you for all that you are and all that you mean to me.

Introduction

Your voice is your most powerful communication tool. It has been with you in its fully developed form since early adulthood. Yet chances are that you may not be conscious of how you actually produce it. Most people don't even know their voices can be changed. When we tell them what our work is, it is common to be met with "Really? A person can change the way he sounds when he talks?"

And why *would* people be aware of this possibility? We don't learn about the voice in school. It certainly isn't a part of routine health-care screenings or education. Presentation training for business rarely includes in-depth voice work, leaving presenters unaware of the dynamic voices they could be using to win their audiences.

Even highly trained voice users such as professional singers usually have not been taught the role of daily speaking in the health and stamina of their singing voices. And many other professional voice users—including teachers, clergy, and politicians—do not give much thought to the manner in which they speak, much less take precautions to prolong the life of their voices and to prevent potentially career-ending vocal injuries. Once hoarseness, throat pain, or vocal fatigue occurs, individuals suddenly become acutely aware of the integral role voice quality plays in communication and find themselves scrambling to learn behaviors and techniques to rehabilitate their voices. As with much of our current health-care system, the voice and vocal health are often overlooked until there is a problem. That's why we're here to represent them!

We were both drawn to voice work from the inside out, as vocal performers ourselves. Through personal experience, we found the relevance, value, mystery, and power of voice compelling enough to study it, research it, teach it, and devote our careers to it. Our goal is to blend the worlds of art and science to create a guide that speaks to both the right and left brain. *The Voice Book* is designed to help you begin (or continue) your journey toward efficient, strong, and effective voice use while minimizing the likelihood of vocal injury and fatigue.

Is This Book for Me?

Some people are drawn to voice work for information about the mechanics of protecting the voice. These folks may have a history of hoarseness or vocal problems, or they may engage in work or play that puts their voice in jeopardy. Other seekers are interested in finding their authentic voice by speaking as well and openly as possible. Whichever category you fall into, this book is for you. The remarkable thing about the process outlined in this book is that it addresses both of those needs. That's what is so amazing about the human body—the most efficient way to use the voice is also the most genuine. So this book is for you if:

- You have ever wanted to change anything about your voice
- Your voice gets hoarse or tired after talking
- You give presentations

- Your work relies on verbal communication (meetings, speeches, etc.)
- You feel your vocal image does not represent you as you wish to be seen
- You talk a lot and want to make sure you can keep doing so
- You use your voice intensely in some way other than speaking (singing, chanting, etc.)
- You want a stronger, fuller voice
- You want to make sure you are speaking as well as you possibly can

Many people think that their voice is an unchangeable feature of their body and their personality. This is simply not true. The voice is a dynamic instrument of the human body and is capable of much more than we think. If you already suffer from vocal fatigue, or if you have had a vocal injury in the past, chances are you are speaking in a way that is inefficient and may not be entirely natural. (Even though your voice may sound and feel natural to you, it is important to recognize the distinction between "natural" and "habitual." We will cover this in greater depth later.) A number of factors influenced the development of your voice. These factors include where you grew up; who your caregivers, role models, and peers were; the overall social climate of your upbringing; and the degree of your vocal awareness and training. No matter what shaped your voice, you can change it.

While this book is a great start, it does not replace work with a qualified voice coach (or therapist if needed). We suggest that you work with the book until you feel you can't get any further on your own. You can use the resources located in the appendix to seek out additional training should you discover vocal problems or have questions not addressed by the book.

Am I a Professional Voice User?

Here is a partial list of occupations whose practitioners are considered professional voice users. Verbal communication is paramount in all these fields. The way you speak affects how well you do your work.

- lawyers
- actors
- teachers
- singers
- choir directors
- clergy
- doctors
- executives
- therapists
- salespeople
- managers
- professional speakers
- magicians
- receptionists
- television news anchors
- politicians
- air traffic contollers
- radio personalities
- auctioneers
- tour guides
- fitness instructors
- entrepreneurs
- traders
- brokers
- marketers
- writers
- real estate developers

What Will I Find in This Book?

The goal of this work is for your voice to function like a well-oiled machine, with little energy loss and minimal wear and tear on the system, so it is useful for you to know the parts of your "machine." If you took violin lessons, you would learn how to take care of your violin—for example, polishing it, not leaving it out in the rain—in addition to learning how to play it. The violin player understands that the quality of the sound depends on both the player and the instrument. Similarly, knowing how the voice system works helps you to use it optimally. To that end, we include information on anatomy and physiology of the various aspects of the speech system. Our intention is to present this information in an understandable way for people without a medical background. Rather than providing an exhaustive review of the anatomy of your vocal mechanism, we will offer what we feel is the most necessary information for optimizing your voice. For those who are interested, chapter 12 goes into further detail.

Speech and voice, although almost always connected, can operate independently from each other. *Voice* refers to the quality or tone of the sounds that you produce. If you open your mouth and hold an *ah* sound, you can hear the basic tone and quality of your voice independent from your articulation. *Speech* refers to the formation of actual words. While clarity of articulation (enunciation, pronunciation, and accent or dialect) is not the focus of this book, we do provide some tips in chapter 7.

The book also includes material on preventing vocal injury. The good news is that there are specific actions that can be taken to safeguard the vocal cords' health. You make decisions every day that can impact the health of your vocal mechanism, and therefore the quality of your instrument. You will learn how to make those decisions wisely.

Vocal image is another concept we explore. Our first impression of people is strongly influenced by how they sound. We make assumptions about people's personalities and character traits based on the way that they speak. Consider the assumptions that you might make about others regarding their intelligence, their levels of education and sophistication, or their social and economic backgrounds based on the sound of their voices and how they articulate. Imagine a woman in business speaking in a loud, harsh manner, and the assumptions that we might make about the way she relates to others. Now consider a woman who speaks in a quiet, small voice, and the assumptions that we might make about her. Not all assumptions are negative, of course. A good orator often appears confidently capable and trustworthy.

Consider also the amount of information we get about a person's state of being from the way she uses her voice. A very brief telephone exchange with someone you know well, even if only the word "hello" is exchanged, can speak volumes about that person's state of being. It is clear whether someone is angry, sad, about to cry, or excited from her tone of voice. Psychologists use voice quality and inflection to help draw conclusions about the psychological state of their patients with regard to depression, mania, and other issues. Much more information is conveyed through the nuances of tone of voice than most people have considered. In fact, well over half of the information that you receive from a speaker comes from variables other than the content of his language. Tone of voice, eye contact, body language, inflection, and other aspects of communication can speak louder than the actual words you choose. Because nonverbal cues carry a good deal of information, it is wise to be aware of how you are using them. Then, to take it a step further, you can let the tone and quality of your voice actively work to your advantage to fully engage your listener. To this end, we include material to help you get the most out of these nonlinguistic elements of speech.

However you use your voice, this book will provide tips and techniques to help you strengthen it, protect it, and make it work for you more effectively.

1

Getting Started

It is helpful to approach this work with playfulness. You can start to create a playful attitude by releasing judgment. This is an opportunity for you to let go of any expectations about your voice and see what it can do above and beyond what it has shown in the past. We tend to have strong feelings about what we are and are not capable of, particularly when it comes to voice. ("I'm tone deaf," "I hate the sound of my voice," and "My voice is shrill" are common declarations of incompetence.) Consider putting those beliefs on hold. You might even replace them with new beliefs that are more positive and accurate. We hope that you will be playful during this exploration and enjoy yourself as you journey through this book.

The most important variable in performing the exercises in this book is *focus*. Most of the exercises are deceptively simple. It is not the action of simply speaking the exercises that is beneficial but rather the way in which you do them and the attention you give them. For most people, achieving the intended behavior initially involves an attention and focus level that we don't necessarily bring to our everyday tasks. This is perhaps the biggest challenge people encounter with voice work and other work involving physical skill. When we first attempt to focus on a singular thought, we find we have several thoughts running through our minds at once. We usually don't concentrate in such a way

Practice Guidelines

(1) Practice in a variety of places. (2) Practice for short periods of time many times throughout the day rather than in one elongated practice session. (3) At first, attend to the exercises with singular focus. (4) Vary your exercises. Don't spend too much time on one exercise.

that we are thinking about only one thing at a time. In fact, our society promotes the opposite: multitasking. When first doing these exercises, however, eliminating distractions and focusing solely on voice are more effective. For example, the car is not the best place to practice this material at first, as your attention will be divided. Specificity of thought aids your ability to attend and focus in this way. As you go through the exercises, keep a single thought, a single focus, a single intention, in the front of your mind at all times.

Unless you have already had voice training or rehabilitation, speaking automatically with little attention paid to how you produce sound is normal. The purpose of voice training or exploration is to lift these automatic behaviors out of the subconscious to "tinker" with them and then allow them to return to the subconscious. The long-term goal is not for you to be excessively aware of your voice to the point of distraction. Rather, let's explore your voice, get to know its nooks and crannies, and develop it so that you have a broader range of colors with which to "paint" when you vocally express yourself.

We are each born with a unique voice. The term *voiceprint* is used to describe the unique, individual character of your voice and how people hear it. Within your voice, however, you have a huge range of dynamic possibilities that, for many speakers, are never explored or integrated into everyday use. The goal of this book isn't to change your voice into somebody else's voice, but rather to optimize and extend your voice. With optimal use, you are able to freely express your own natural sound in any way you wish.

When you work through the book, be patient and kind to yourself. It can be frustrating for some people (especially those of us with perfectionist tendencies) to understand something intellectually but still be unable to "do it right." This is the other major challenge with voice work. Because you may have spent your entire life using your speaking voice in a particular manner, the vocal benefit from this program will develop *over time* rather than overnight. This is because, as we mentioned before and will mention again, most of our voice and speech characteristics are maintained through habit. Habit kills choice and variety. Fortunately, although habits are powerful and ingrained, all it really takes to change a vocal habit is knowledge, attention, and repetition. We believe that the difficulty of breaking an interfering vocal habit isn't necessarily the habit itself but rather the amount of attention it takes to bring that habitual behavior into awareness and then make a different choice. Releasing the perception that "habits die hard" will make it easier to let them go.

Many of us have habits that interfere with a free, natural voice by promoting tension and constriction in the vocal mechanism. If you are like a lot of us, you might unwittingly hold chronic tension in your jaw, throat, and neck because of experiences throughout your lifetime. We usually develop physical and vocal habits that reflect what we think is appropriate in a given environment. For example, if your mother or father said children should be seen but not heard, it is possible that you might have some tension in your jaw and throat born out of your childhood attempt to "hold back" your speech to please your caregivers. This "holding back" of your voice and speech can remain present in your adult voice if it goes unchecked. In other words, perceived judgment about our voice contributes to the way it develops. Some adults remember being asked in choir to just "move their lips" rather than sing. This seemingly small criticism can contribute to poor vocal self-esteem and may introduce a hesitation to the voice that carries over into other aspects of life.

Also, some people who undergo emotional, sexual, or physical trauma may acquire tension in their speech system resulting in vocal changes. If you have a history of trauma that you feel is affecting your ability to access your voice, you may consider addressing this issue with a professional psychologist or psychiatrist to facilitate better release of your muscles. Some people find that when they release their abdominal muscles with breathing exercises, or release muscles in the throat or jaw by doing voice work, they feel an emotional rush. Usually an emotional rush is interpreted as "I am about to cry right now" or "I am about to laugh" or "I am about to yell." If you notice such a sensation, we encourage you to experience that rush without judgment.

Using the Audio CD

The audio CD that accompanies this book is designed to improve your understanding of the concepts and exercises. Just as a picture is worth a thousand words, a sound, in the case of voice training, is priceless. Much of the material in this book will come to life with the CD. The material can be uploaded to your computer and transferred to an MP3 player to optimize portability.

We encourage you to listen to tracks 1 and 2 before reading the book, as they provide a brief introduction as well as a fun ear training exercise. You will know when to listen to tracks 3 through 11 by looking for the CD icon pictured above when it appears throughout the book. When you see the icon, we recommend that you read or skim through the material first, then listen to the appropriate track, as indicated by the number inside the icon.

Within each set of exercises in the text, you'll find additional exercises and extra practice material not included on the CD. Please keep this in mind if you choose to use the book and CD simultaneously.

One Last Note

Even though the exercises in this book are safe for individuals with vocal injury, they are by no means designed to replace vocal rehabilitation and care that you would get from an ear, nose, and throat physician and speech pathologist. While both authors of this book are licensed speech pathologists and much of the information contained within is from a medical perspective, the authors assume that you are approaching the work with injury-free vocal cords. If you have concerns about the health of your voice as you work through this book, please consult an appropriate medical professional as described in chapters 10 and 12.

2

Opening the Channel: Alignment

The Alexander Technique, a beautiful movement system for train-ing alignment, was created by an actor who repeatedly lost his voice and realized one day that he had significant alignment prob-lems. *Alignment*, for our purposes, refers to the relationship of the head to the rest of the body. When he allowed his body to return to proper alignment, his voice problems vanished. While the solu-tion is not so simple for every voice problem, alignment does play a significant role in many voice issues.

A theater major was referred for voice therapy because she repeatedly "lost her voice" during rehearsals and performance. On evaluation it was apparent that when she performed, she significantly misaligned her head, jutting her chin forward and raising it a little. This was pointed out to her during the evalu-ation, and some exercises were offered to adjust her alignment. Several months after her single session, her referring teacher reported that the student had no further voice issues.

In another scenario, an at-home mom came for voice ther-apy because she had pain in her throat when she talked. Her vocal mechanism was evaluated by an ear, nose, and throat physician and determined to be normal. Her posture, however, was char-acterized by slumped shoulders (possibly impeding good breath access for speech) as well as a habitual misalignment of her head and neck. It appeared that the way she connected with her kids involved jutting her chin forward to "reach" them. During treatment sessions, she learned to play on the floor, read books, do "funny voices," and interact without compromising her alignment. While therapy also addressed issues of breath and resonance, the adjustments in alignment were the primary aids to the elimination of her pain.

Free Your Neck and the Rest Will Follow

Voice quality and ease, or the lack thereof, is closely linked to posture and muscle tension. Slouching posture or tension in the throat, jaw, shoulders, and neck can negatively affect the voice. Therefore, we will start our journey to vocal efficiency by first addressing body alignment.

Heads are heavy (15 pounds or so), and the human body is designed such that the bones of the skeleton support the weight of the head. However, many of us don't have a sufficiently straight carriage, or posture, to allow the head to be fully supported by the bones of the skeleton. Therefore, we have to overuse neck muscles to support the weight of the head. This state is called *misalignment* and can create several negative repercussions for voice quality and comfort.

One vocal consequence of misalignment is extraneous tension in the muscles of the neck, which then creates tension in the vocal system. Another issue is the contraction of muscles at the back of the neck and the base of the skull. Keep in mind that muscles shorten when they contract. Most people unknowingly contract and shorten muscles at the back of the neck and base of the skull, thereby causing misalignment. Tension in these muscles not only creates discomfort (this is an area of tightness for many people), but can also create tension in the jaw, because tension in the back of the body tends to lead to corresponding tension in the front. Therefore, misalignment of the head can easily lead to jaw tension (figure 2-1), which negatively affects voice by constricting the channel through which the voice flows.

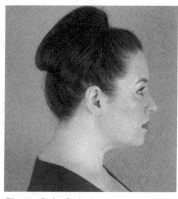

Figure 2-1: Chin jut

Yet another effect of misalignment is related to the shape of the *vocal tract* (figure 2-2), which is the tube that runs from the larynx to the lips and includes the throat, mouth, and nose. If the head is misaligned, the vocal tract's shape is distorted in a way that is disadvantageous for voice. The vocal tract is essentially a built-in amplifier that makes your voice louder and more resonant if you don't constrict it. By misaligning the head, we basically unplug the amplifier and cut out many of the acoustic benefits of the vocal tract. Therefore, proper head alignment can not only reduce laryngeal tension, but can also improve vocal projection and reduce vocal effort. More information about the mechanics of alignment can be found in chapter 12.

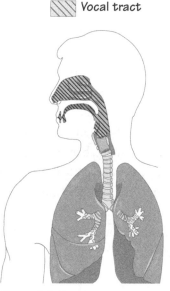

Figure 2-2: Vocal tract

Alignment as Habit

Much of voice work has the single goal of identifying habit and replacing it with choice. Arthur Lessac, an eminent voice trainer, said, "Habit is an anesthetic." This is particularly relevant for voice as, for most of us, our speaking style has been habituated. Everything we do habitually we tend to do without awareness; that is what makes it a habit. Voice training is intended to create awareness of actions and behaviors that have been habitual up to this point. This is a challenging task because habit is powerful. For example, the way you hold your head and jaw is often difficult to change at first because it involves wrapping your mind around the concepts that (a) these muscles exist in the first place; (b) you may be holding them with quite a bit of tension; (c) there is something you can do about that; and (d) this is desirable and worthwhile! We encourage you to repeatedly check in with yourself for habitual behaviors and replace them with behaviors of your choosing. We will be guiding you to do so as we progress through the program.

We also need to differentiate between natural and habitual. Have you ever carried a really heavy shopping bag that cut into your fingers so much that your fingers felt stuck in that position when you put the bag down? When that happens to us, it actually hurts in the beginning to release the fingers. That doesn't mean that the stuck, bent fingers are in the natural position. It means they have habituated to that position, and one of the reasons it is uncomfortable to move them is because you are releasing tension. This may also be the case with trying new alignment. Keep this in mind as you work through these exercises and begin to change your habits.

Exercises to Explore Alignment

Rest Position

Let's begin with bringing your upper body into alignment. Start either standing or seated comfortably with your back straight, not leaning back against anything. Lift your shoulders up to your ears as far as they will go. Squeeze your shoulder blades together behind you then drop your shoulders down—heavy and hard (figure 2-3).

Make sure your arms and upper chest are relaxed, and relax your shoulders without letting them roll forward. This movement sequence puts your shoulders into a position of alignment, which is necessary in order for the head and neck to be aligned. Next, bring your head into a centered position so that it is balanced evenly over the top of your body. Your ear lobes are over your shoulders, your chin is level, and the crown of your head is the highest point on your body. It may feel like you are pulling your chin in a little bit or that you are looking down a little bit relative to your baseline position. That is OK. As you experience this new alignment, take note of any holding patterns that you might be developing. Your head should feel light and free rather than held in one position. This is a dynamic posture meant to facilitate

Figure 2-3: Shoulders up, back, and down

relaxed, fluid movement of your body, rather than a static posture. If you feel as though you are standing like a statue, release your body further still. Check the rest of your body (feet, legs, buttocks, belly, hands, forehead, etc.) for any tension to be released. As you maintain the aligned position, allow your head to feel light, and imagine that it is actually floating up from your spine.

Try imagining that you have a string running from the crown of your head to the ceiling, and that the string gives a gentle pull upward on the crown of your head like a marionette's string. Some people feel that a pressure in the back of their neck is relieved as they mentally lighten the weight of their head and allow their head to be supported by an imaginary string from above.

Remember that the spine ends higher in the head than most of us think. It actually goes all the way up into the brain stem and ends not at the neck, but rather in the center of the head. One purpose of alignment is to allow energy to move freely up and down the spine, the railroad track of nerves and energy in the body. So we want to hold the head in such a way that the upper spine doesn't kink but rather points straight up at the sky.

Now that your head is aligned, let's relax the jaw. Keeping your lips gently touching, allow your jaw to release so that there is a little bit of space between your upper and lower back teeth. You don't need to actively open your jaw; just let it hang heavy, as though there are weights attached to your jawbone causing it to hang comfortably and heavily.

Now, observe your tongue. Allow your tongue to lie flat, down, and back like a rug on the floor of your mouth, with the tip behind the lower front teeth. Observe a feeling of space in the back of the mouth that is probably not usually present. Make sure your lips are closed. You also want to make sure that your eyes are alive and active and that your face is engaged and relaxed. Check your forehead to make sure that you are not furrowing your brow as you concentrate.

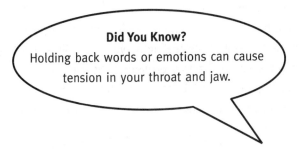

Did You Know?
Holding back words or emotions can cause tension in your throat and jaw.

This position (head aligned, jaw released, and tongue flat) is the natural resting position (figure 2-4). This assertion may come as a surprise because it is not the habitual resting position for

Figure 2-4: Rest position

most of us. It is, however, the position that uses the least effort. If you can separate mental effort from physical effort, you can feel that this is a physically easy position once you get used to it. It may feel uncomfortable in the beginning because it is unusual for most people.

Most of us tend to carry our tongues plastered against the roof of our mouths or against the top front teeth. So this position of the lowered tongue is for many the most challenging aspect of this trinity of head, jaw, and tongue release.

Now let's take a look at how alignment affects sound. Purposefully misalign your head now. Jut your head forward or your chin up; shorten the muscles in the back of your neck slightly. Register the feeling of this position. Now bring your head back into alignment. Observe the feeling of *this* position. Now misalign, and now bring it back into alignment. Get used to moving between these states. Take a deep breath and say *ah* for a long time. While you sustain this sound, move your head in and out of alignment. Observe how the sound changes with your head position. Notice both the sound and the feeling as you move in and out of alignment while sustaining this *ah* sound. Usually, when the head is misaligned, our sound becomes slightly pinched and flat. With alignment, we usually hear improved resonance and "roundness" in the voice.

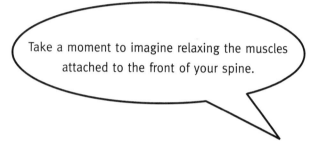

Take a moment to imagine relaxing the muscles attached to the front of your spine.

The rest position, then, is: head aligned, jaw released, tongue down and back. There is no need to rigidly maintain this position; that would create a new set of tense muscles. As the Alexander Technique reminds us, alignment is a journey, not a destination.

The road to maintaining alignment is to gently invite your body to come into this position throughout the day and become aware of any tension you may hold in the muscles of the neck, jaw, and tongue. Because remembering to use these new behaviors is often the hardest part of integrating them, you might want to include visual reminders (such as sticky notes on your computer) in your environment to cue you.

Wall Exercise

Stand with your back against a wall. Allow your feet to be under your hips. Unlock your knees. As you are standing against the wall, bring your attention to the places where the back of the body is in contact with the wall (figure 2-5).

Figure 2-5: Wall exercise

Walk your feet forward and allow your knees to bend so that you are leaning a bit against the wall. Align your head such that your entire upper back and the back of your head come into contact with the wall. For most people, it will involve a pulling inward of the chin to get the head all along the wall. Feel this stretch and elongation. Make sure you don't choke yourself. Carefully walk your feet back under your body and walk away from the wall maintaining your new alignment.

Shoulder Blade Squeeze

Here is another way to achieve upper body alignment. Stand with your feet under your hips and your knees unlocked. Spread your arms out on either side of your body at shoulder height with your palms facing the ceiling (figure 2-6).

Allow your shoulders to drop away from your ears while maintaining this arm position and palm position. Make sure your

Figure 2-6: Shoulder blade squeeze

thumbs are really twisted all the way around so that your palms are facing up, parallel with the ceiling. Bring your attention to the space between your shoulder blades. While keeping your shoulder blades slightly together and your shoulders dropped, allow your arms to return to a rest position. Look at a full-length mirror to make sure your shoulders are dropped and even. Feel the openness in your chest as you walk, sit, and even dance.

Stretching the Head and Neck

Clasp your hands together behind your head to cradle the base of your skull—not your neck, but the base of your skull (figure 2-7). Now do an isometric exercise by pushing back against your hands with your head. (*Isometric* means that once you find the

position, you hold still and press instead of moving.) Tuck your chin in slightly and "lead" with the muscles that join the upper back-of-neck to the base of the skull. Those are the muscles that are engaged.

Figure 2-7: Cradling the skull base

Keep everything that is not involved with this activity relaxed. Relax the jaw, relax the upper chest, and make sure that you breathe. Hold this position with significant pressure for about 30 seconds. When you are finished, inhale and let your hands go at the same time. Very often you will feel a little head rush as the blood moves through the capillaries at the back of the neck.

Should you desire additional practice with alignment, we encourage you to explore other methods or practices of posture optimization such as the Alexander Technique, the Feldenkrais Method, or yoga.

Frequently Asked Questions about Alignment

Q: *You say this is natural, yet I feel uncomfortable. How can that be?*

A: We return again to the difference between natural and habitual. Just because something is natural does not mean it is habitual. And if you try to do something that is not habitual, no matter how natural it is, it potentially will feel uncomfortable in the beginning. At the same time, if you are feeling real pain and a sense of tension in this position, you may be holding it with too much force or have a physical obstacle to alignment.

Q: *I feel like I have to tense my tongue to keep it down. What do I do?*

A: First of all, congratulations! We are very glad that you have enough awareness of your actions and body to feel that your tongue is actually being held down instead of being allowed to relax on the floor of your mouth. It takes awareness and consciousness, but with practice you will achieve a sensation of your tongue lying on the floor of your mouth like a rug without feeling like you are pushing it or pulling it into position. In the beginning, however, it is often necessary to place the tongue in that position, and once it is there, allow it to relax.

Q: *With my new posture, I feel like I am looking down. Am I doing it right?*

A: Yes, you probably are. Most of us misalign our heads by looking up slightly. It trains our eyes to always look down, because if your head is tilted upward and your eyes are neutral, you would be looking up at the ceiling most of the time. So if you bring your head into this new alignment and your eyes don't shift, you are, indeed, looking at the floor. In addition to retraining the head, neck, jaw, and tongue, you will also actually be retraining your eyes to look straight ahead instead of down your nose. Bet you didn't think voice work would involve your eyes!

Q: *Do I look like I have a double chin?*

A: Most likely, yes. In fact, one reason that we develop a chin-jut posture is probably to overcome the self-consciousness that comes with the perception that we have a double chin. Deal with it. Voice work is about uncovering habitual tension that interferes with a free, strong, healthy voice. Making friends with your real jaw line is just an added bonus.

3

Summoning the Power: Breath

Breathing well can play a large role not only in voice quality but also in quality of life. An older woman was seen for voice therapy because for more than two years she had had pain when talking, vocal hoarseness and weakness, and a loss of singing ability. It became clear in therapy that her recent history of caring for her dying husband and ill sister had affected her breathing as well as her outlook. Even though she knew how to use deep breathing for singing, she realized she was not implementing this knowledge. She also realized that her body had developed tension that inhibited her breath as a result of her emotional pain. Therapy focused on breath work to support her voice and also to allow her to let go of some of the physical and emotional tension that she had accumulated. Her voice as well as her overall outlook improved as a result.

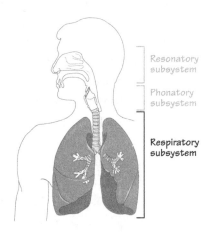

Resonatory subsystem

Phonatory subsystem

Respiratory subsystem

Another client, this one with chronic asthma, came for vocal coaching because she felt her voice was weak and quiet, and her throat got tired after a short conversation. Probably because of her asthma, her breathing was high in the chest and shallow. She was not getting enough breath for efficient speech, and the way she breathed caused tension in her neck and throat muscles. She was initially resistant to the work prescribed because she had breathed inefficiently for so long that she couldn't believe that her breathing could possibly improve. After a few sessions focusing on breathing exercises, she was shocked by her ability to breathe deeply and easily despite her asthma. She found her overall comfort throughout the day increased, her need for rescue inhalers decreased dramatically, her ability to exercise improved, and her voice quality improved. Specifically, her voice had more power and resonance and she had no discomfort with prolonged speaking. She credited the improvements to breath work.

Through the years of rehabilitating injured voices, we have found that individuals who are informed about the inner workings of their voice are more likely to incorporate a practice of vocal health into their lives. It is easier to make daily decisions about vocal health if you understand the principles than if you simply follow a list of dos and don'ts. However, we do not want to overwhelm you with extensive information about the anatomy and physiology of breathing. To strike a balance, we provide a basic description of optimal speech breathing in the paragraphs that follow. If you would like a more thorough explanation of respiratory mechanics, see chapter 12.

Breath is integral to voice production; vocal folds cannot vibrate without it. For our purposes, we separate voice production into three discrete yet interdependent subsystems (figure 3-1). These are the respiratory system (lungs), the phonatory system (larynx), and the resonatory system (vocal tract).

This chapter focuses on the respiratory system—the basic anatomy and physiology of breath movement. Chapter 4 focuses on the larynx—what it looks like, what it is made of, and how it works. Chapter 5 is dedicated to the vocal tract and how it is used to resonate the vibrating column of air produced by the first two systems.

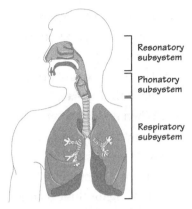

Figure 3-1: The three subsystems of speech production

Building a Case for Low Breathing

Babies tend to breathe using the expansion of the lower thoracic cavity, and allowing expansion in the low belly. However, as we get older, many of us begin to breathe high in the chest. Perhaps we become more body conscious and don't want to allow our abdomen to move outward as we inhale. For some of us, breath becomes high and shallow due to numerous factors including stress, anxiety, and behaviors learned from seeing the way others breathe.

Low breathing is the most efficient way to breathe for life, speech, and song. In fact, an examination of the anatomy associated with breathing suggests that our bodies are designed to breathe lower rather than higher in the torso.

• Lungs are pear shaped (bigger at the bottom than at the top). There are more air sacs in the lower lungs, thus more room for air than in the upper lungs.

- The lower rib cage has more expandability than the upper rib cage because of the floating ribs and the flexible cartilage. It can therefore create more space for air.
- The lungs expand primarily in a downward direction when they inflate.
- When the *diaphragm* (the floor of the thorax) contracts, it lowers and flattens. It also pushes the abdominal contents down and out, giving the impression of "breathing into the stomach." The belly is designed to soften, allowing for this expansion. This makes room for the lower lungs to expand more than the upper lungs.
- Expanding the upper thorax involves using the chest, shoulder, neck, and jaw muscles to try to lift the entire upper rib cage, resulting in a minuscule amount of room for the tiny upper lungs to expand.
- The back muscles over the kidneys are able to give slightly when the diaphragm lowers. Therefore, when one breathes deeply, the lower lungs are able to expand in all directions.
- Form follows function. Breathing for speech isn't necessarily the same as breathing for sprinting, swimming, or even sleeping. What we *do* with the air ideally dictates how we bring it into the body. Breathing for speech involves voluntary control of inhalation and exhalation. After inhaling as much air as we need to say whatever it is we want to say, we then volitionally control the air as it leaves the body and is turned into voice. By breathing lower in the body, we are better able to control exhalation for speech, singing, or even playing an instrument by using the abdominal muscles.

Exercises to Explore Breathing   4

Because breath control is such an important aspect of voice production, and because it is not habitual for many people, a variety
of exercises are included for breathing exploration. These exercises
are designed to help you learn to breathe deeply, with ease and
comfort, and to help you capitalize on the body's natural ability to
breathe without tension.

Increasing Awareness

Awareness comes before change. So without changing your breathing, sit in a comfortable, unslumped position. Place one hand on
your belly and one hand on your chest. Close your eyes. Let your
hands be curious and notice what is happening in your body as
you inhale and exhale. Notice the depth, rhythm, and rate of your
breathing. Notice what parts of the body move when you breathe
and what parts don't. Notice how much, if any, resistance is associated with breathing.

Fff Exercise

Take in a breath any way you feel comfortable. Sustain a *fff* sound
as though you have a slow leak, and exhale all of your air in this
manner. Feel that, as you run out of breath, your stomach moves
inward to help push the air out. When you start to run out of air,
purposely pull your stomach in, squeezing the breath out from your
lower abdomen as if you are squeezing toothpaste out from the
bottom of the tube.

When you feel that your lungs are empty, like two shriveled
little balloons, and your stomach is pulled in, pause for a moment

Figure 3-2: Abdomen pulled in for exhalation

Figure 3-3: Abdomen released for inhalation

and just be present with that feeling of wanting to breathe without actually breathing (figure 3-2). Then allow your abdominal muscles to release and "pop" out. (You have to be willing to let your stomach pooch out in order to breathe properly!) When your abdominal muscles release and your stomach pops out, air is sucked into your lungs as a result of the vacuum that you have created (figure 3-3). Repeat this exercise three times.

If you have ever squeezed too much lotion or shampoo out of a bottle and tried to suck it back in, you've demonstrated this principle. The first thing you do is squeeze the extra air out of the bottle, thereby creating a vacuum. Then you release the bottle, and it slurps in the material in front of the opening because of the vacuum that has been created. This is the same principle that works in our lungs.

Lower Rib Side Breathing

Put your hands on the sides of your lower rib cage just above your waist. As you inhale, breathe into your lower ribs so that they push your hands out to the side (figure 3-4).

As you exhale, feel the lower ribs move all the way in toward your center. Continue to inhale and exhale, feeling the expansion and contraction of the lower ribs. Aim to isolate the sides of your body so that your breath doesn't feel like it is going into your chest or stomach but only goes into your sides.

Figure 3-4: Feeling lower side rib expansion during inhalation

Now stretch over to one side with your arm reaching over your head (figure 3-5). Breathe into the side of your body that is stretched in this position. Come back up to standing, breathe into your sides, and notice whether you feel more expansion in the side you just stretched. Repeat on the other side.

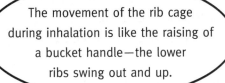

The movement of the rib cage during inhalation is like the raising of a bucket handle—the lower ribs swing out and up.

Figure 3-5: Stretching to the side while breathing deeply

Back Expansion Breathing

One way to feel lower back expansion during inhalation is by wrapping your arms around your torso and giving yourself a big hug (figure 3-6). Slightly bend your knees and bend over, releasing your neck so your head hangs freely. As you are in this bent-over position, feel yourself breathing into the area of your back around your kidneys (between your ribs and your hips). Drop your arms and roll up one vertebra at a time, allowing your head

Figure 3-6: Opening the back during inhalation

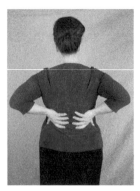

Figure 3-7: Feeling back expansion during inhalation

to be the last thing up. While you roll up, maintain the feeling of expansion in your lower back during inhalation.

Another way to feel back expansion during breathing is to place your hands at your waist so that your fingertips are touching each other along your spine. Your hands are between your ribs and hips (figure 3-7). Start with an exhale, and then as you inhale, become aware of the expansion of your back. Your fingertips will separate slightly from each other during your inhale, and as you exhale, your fingertips will come back together.

Breathing with Speech

We are now going to use the same principle as in the *fff* exercise and apply it to speech. The intention here is to capitalize on the body's ability to suck in air without our "help." Just as with the *fff*, exhale all your air to depletion, but instead of using the *fff* sound to get rid of the air, count aloud as long as you can on one breath, feeling your abdomen move in as you do so. Vary the pitch so that your counting resembles conversational speech, and blend the numbers fluidly without rushing. As you use your breath by counting, your volume will drop off unless you keep it steady—avoid fading out and make the last number of the breath as loud as the first.

As you get to the end of your breath, you will need to move your stomach inward intentionally. After you are out of breath, pause for a moment and don't breathe. Then let your abdomen pop out and let the air get sucked into your lungs. It may feel as if a balloon is quickly expanding in your belly. Continue counting from where you left off. Repeat for three breath cycles.

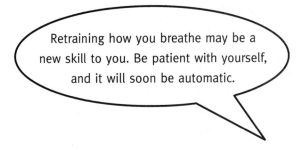

Retraining how you breathe may be a new skill to you. Be patient with yourself, and it will soon be automatic.

Candle Blowing

Place one hand on your upper chest and one hand on your belly. Take in a breath in any way that feels comfortable to you. Next, blow out all of your breath quickly as though you were blowing out candles on a cake. When you have blown out every molecule of air that you possibly can, pause for a moment, allowing a vacuum to be created. Then simultaneously release your belly and inhale. Notice the sensation that you are bringing air into your belly, creating a "belly breath."

Repeat this exercise several times until you are able to feel a connection between the release of your belly and the inhalation of air.

Pant from the Abdomen

Put your hand on your belly and pant like a puppy from your abdomen. As you pant, feel your belly pulsing inward as you exhale. As you release your belly in between each pant to inhale, feel your belly expand outward.

Sniff and Blow

Slowly draw in air through your nose. Feel your abdomen, ribs, and back expand to accept the air. Blow out through your mouth slowly and comfortably. Every time you repeat the exercise, sniff in a little faster each time. Decrease the amount of time it takes you to inhale while maintaining your connection with your new expanded belly.

Interestingly enough, when people sniff in, the vocal cords fly apart and come into a full V position, allowing for the maximum amount of air to rush by them (see figure 4-1 in the next chapter). See if you can visualize your vocal cords coming widely apart as you repeat the Sniff and Blow exercise.

Sometimes the Sniff and Blow exercise helps restore the larynx to a relaxed state should it spasm (such as in a coughing spell).

Exhale Your Voice

Release your belly and draw in a breath either through your nose or mouth. Place your hand in front of your mouth with your palm facing you. Sustain an *ooo* vowel sound into your palm at a comfortable pitch. Notice the gentle stream of air being exhaled as you produce voice. If your vocal cords close too tightly, you may not feel any air on your hand. Try relaxing your throat and exhaling more breath as you make sound. By doing this exercise correctly, you learn to produce sound without overtensing your vocal cords. The ultimate goal is not to have a breathy voice but to avoid squeezing the vocal cords together too hard.

Pulse Sounds

Put a hand on your stomach and forcefully make a *F!* sound. Do this three times. Now forcefully make a *V!* sound. As you make this sound, feel your stomach move in toward your spine. Then, still feeling that pulling inward of your stomach, say, "Voo, vee, vie, vay." Make sure there is no pressure in your throat and that the sound you are making isn't breathy or strained.

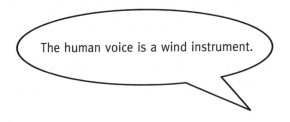

The human voice is a wind instrument.

Deep Breathing

Keep one hand on your stomach and one hand on your chest and sit comfortably with your eyes closed. Take a slow, deep breath that involves your stomach moving outward as you inhale and moving inward as you exhale. It is as though the center, or core, of your being opens up and expands in all directions to receive the breath and closes inward to expel the breath. Take two to three minutes to breathe in this manner. Incidentally, this is an excellent "stress buster" in moments of anxiety.

Frequently Asked Questions about Breathing

Q: *What is the best way to practice breathing?*

A: It is usually easiest for people to make changes by practicing for short periods numerous times throughout the day in a number of different settings. For example, it is better to practice your breathing for 30 seconds at the top of every hour as you go through your day than to set aside 15 minutes a day to practice in the morning. Practicing in this spread-out fashion will increase the likelihood that your new breathing will become habitual.

That being said, when you are first acquiring the skill of low breathing, there is benefit to spending several minutes at a time practicing. As with anything new, it will take attention and time to do it properly. You need to invest this focused time to learn at the beginning. Once you have the muscle memory for this breathing, you will be able to multitask and do other things while you practice. As was previously noted, initial practice requires a single focus in order to cement new skills, but once the skills have been acquired, it is necessary to multitask in order to mimic the complexity of everyday life.

Q: *My stomach wants to move in while I breathe in. Is there something wrong with me?*

A: No, that is very common. This is called *paradoxical breathing*. A lot of people think that breathing means sucking the stomach in and lifting the chest up. If this is your habitual pattern of breathing, don't worry. Your breath will return to its natural state with practice.

One of the most important things that you can do is to remember to maintain a soft belly. If you are sucking your belly in as you inhale, there is a possibility that you are chronically holding your belly in through tension. You also might be lifting your chest and shoulders when you inhale. Spending several moments throughout your day allowing the stomach to pooch slightly as you inhale, while keeping your chest and shoulders relaxed, might help you to coordinate your new breathing method.

Q: *Why can I do this lying down but not sitting up?*

A: When you are lying on your back, gravity helps to pull your abdomen toward your spine as you breathe out, thereby assisting this new breathing pattern. Also, when we lie down, we relax, and the body tends to revert to its natural state. It is also almost impossible to lift the shoulders and upper chest when lying down, which is a common mistake that people make when breathing standing up.

Try breathing while lying on your back to train your body to breathe abdominally. Then, as an intermediate step between lying down and standing up, breathe in this new manner while sitting. You may also want to examine your posture. If your midsection is slouched, the diaphragm can't contract optimally and the belly can't expand well. Aim to sit in a straight, yet relaxed, position.

Q: *I notice that when I am anxious, my breathing is fast and high. Why is this?*

A: Anxiety and stress can trigger the "fight or flight" response of the autonomic nervous system. Breathing becomes shallower and faster to prepare your body to fight or run away. This system also works in the other direction: high, fast breathing can send signals to your body that you are anxious or in danger (whether you are or not). Many of us carry such unexamined tension that we go through the day with our bodies believing that we are in this state of desperate arousal. Many stress management programs teach deep breathing as a primary technique for stress reduction and relaxation. Just as high, tight breathing will tell your body you are in danger, low and relaxed breathing will tell your body you are not in danger and you can relax.

Q: *Should I breathe through my nose or my mouth?*

A: There is a time and a place for both. When you are breathing for relaxation or stress reduction, it is usually recommended that you breathe in through your nose. The small hairs in your nose filter out impurities in the air, and the moisture in your nose humidifies the air as it passes through. For speech, however, we tend to breathe in through the mouth because it is faster. When you are practicing these exercises, it is recommended that you do both. Breathe in through your nose during the deep breathing exercises and through your mouth for the speech exercises.

Q: *When will this become natural?*

A: It is already natural. Your question really is, when will this become *habitual*? While this may seem like an annoying semantic distinction, the words we use reflect our thinking and therefore our behavior. Breathing in this manner may not be habitual for you yet, but we have demonstrated that it is the body's natural mechanism. Therefore, replacing habit with conscious behavior is the goal. That being said, it takes surprisingly little time to habituate the natural breathing pattern. After a month or two of consistent practice, your body will gravitate toward the less effortful form of breathing outlined above.

Q: *Why bother? I can already breathe.*

A: Yes, indeed, you can already breathe. However, if you are like most people in our society, you may be breathing in a high, tight, shallow fashion that reflects our busy schedules and tight clothing, and this does not provide as much oxygen as your body would really like. If you use the techniques described to get adequate oxygen, your breathing sends a message to your body saying that you are in a relaxed and anxiety-free state. Also, healthy, optimal, efficient voicing requires a little more breath than many people tend to use. Consider the possibility that there is benefit to going beyond the breathing patterns that are habitual to you.

Q: *I get light-headed during these exercises. Is this OK?*

A: No worries. Most likely you have caused a temporary disruption in the balance between carbon dioxide and oxygen. While disconcerting, the light-headedness from deep breathing is usually not harmful. If you become light-headed, look at your hand, pick a point on the palm, and stare at it for a moment. The light-headedness will begin to pass. Do not be concerned if light-headedness occurs; try decreasing the amount of air you are exchanging while still releasing your abdomen when you inhale. Work within your comfort zone. If it persists for more than a few minutes after the exercises end, it is caused by something other than the exercises and may require medical attention.

Q: *Will low breathing cause my belly to get bigger over time?*

A: Nope. Allowing your abdominal wall to move in and out naturally simply increases its range of motion. If, however, you are used to holding your stomach in, it might feel like it is bigger when you allow it to move freely.

4

Bringing Sound to Life: The Vocal Cords

To create the speaking voice, 18 small muscles in and around the larynx rapidly contract and release in a coordinated pattern controlled subconsciously by the brain. Sometimes certain muscles can tighten too much while others don't work hard enough. This can happen for a number of reasons, including talking when the vocal folds are injured or holding tension and anxiety in the throat.

A woman sought a voice evaluation because she had been severely hoarse for six years. She had seen a multitude of medical specialists and was diagnosed with a neurological voice disorder called spasmodic dysphonia. She was referred to us for Botox injections to treat it. On our further examination

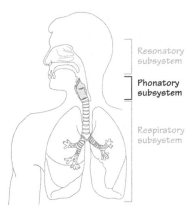

Resonatory subsystem

Phonatory subsystem

Respiratory subsystem

of her voice, we determined that her problem was one of chronic laryngeal tension rather than spasmodic dysphonia. In other words, she had learned to squeeze the muscles around her vocal cords so hard that she wasn't able to get her voice out clearly.

Because most individuals have little awareness of their laryngeal muscles, this squeezing of the larynx can become habitual and "normal." Moreover, when an individual's voice is chronically hoarse, a natural response is to try to push the voice out, resulting in even more constriction and a worsening of vocal quality. Over time, this individual seemed to forget how to produce her voice without pushing, straining, or squeezing her laryngeal muscles. After 15 minutes of laryngeal massage and vocal exercises, her voice returned to normal, and she required no further treatment. This poignant account of tension and strain in the larynx certainly demonstrates the most extreme side of laryngeal tension, yet it reminds us that we can subconsciously tighten the muscles that control our voices, thereby causing difficulty with vocal access, comfort, and quality.

In another case, a secretary for a medical office got a cold and laryngitis. She returned to work before she was recovered and continued her duties answering phones. Instead of improving, her hoarseness got worse until, two months later, she was about to go on disability because of her voice. It turned out that her vocal cords actually did heal, but she had compensated for the laryngitis by squeezing her throat muscles and was continuing to do so out of habit. After four sessions of voice therapy focusing on alignment, breathing, resonance, and releasing the throat muscles, her voice was back to normal.

Your Larynx and You

The second subsystem of voice is the *phonatory system*, which makes sound through the use of the vocal folds. Here we take you on a brief tour of the system. (More detailed information is found in chapter 12.) There are two true vocal folds in your larynx (LAR-inks), which is sometimes also called the voice box or the Adam's apple. The larynx sits right on top of the airway (trachea).

The two vocal folds run from front to back in the body. If you look down at them from the top of your throat, they look like a V with the point of the V at the front of the neck (figure 4-1).

Throughout the book, we use the terms *vocal cords* and *vocal folds* interchangeably. While most people are familiar with the term *vocal cords*, the technical term is *vocal folds*. The nomenclature is relevant because the term *cords* implies that the vibration of the vocal cords is what makes sound, making us string instruments. This is not true, however. The vocal folds' vibration (opening and closing repeatedly) valves the breath, which in turn makes the sound. This is why we are wind instruments.

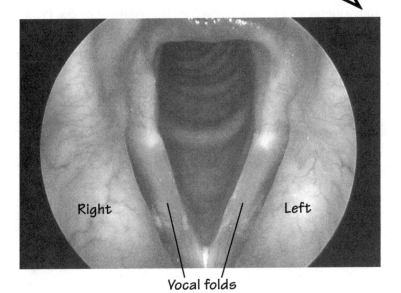

Figure 4-1: Open vocal folds (Courtesy Kay Pentax)

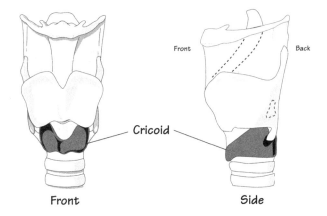

Figure 4-2: Cricoid cartilage

The larynx is made up of separate cartilaginous structures that are held together with muscle and covered with tissue. The top ring of the trachea is also the bottom of the larynx. This ring is called the *cricoid* (CRY-koid) *cartilage.* It is shaped like a signet ring with the narrow side facing forward and the wide side facing backward (figure 4-2).

On the top of the cricoid cartilage in the front of your neck rests the *thyroid cartilage* (figure 4-3). The hard part of your

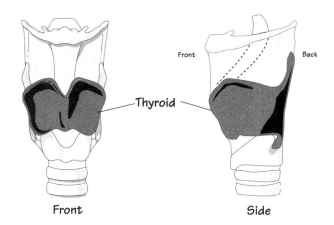

Figure 4-3: Thyroid cartilage

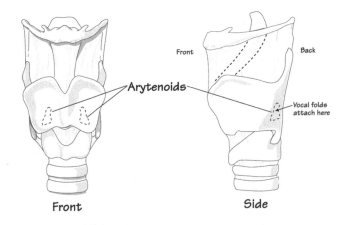

Figure 4-4: Arytenoid cartilages

Adam's apple that you can feel from the outside is called the *thyroid lamina*. The word *thyroid* comes from the Latin word for "shield," and that is exactly what those hard structures are doing: shielding your vocal cords. There are two thyroid laminae that are fused at an angle in the front of your neck, creating a hard wall around the front and sides of your vocal folds. You can feel the place where your thyroid laminae are fused together by touching the pointy part of your Adam's apple. The dent at the top of this place is called the *thyroid notch*. The angle at which the thyroid laminae are fused is narrow in men and wide in women. This is why men's Adam's apples tend to be more prominent than women's. We'll come back to the thyroid notch in a moment. But first, let's explore the back of the larynx.

Remember that the wide side of the cricoid ring is in the back. Right on top of the wide part of the cricoid ring sit two small structures side by side, like two birds perched on a telephone wire. These structures are also made of cartilage and are shaped like pyramids (figure 4-4). They are called *arytenoids* (uh-RIH-tuh-noids). The arytenoids are quite flexible, as the muscles that connect them to the cricoid and to each other allow them to move together or apart, to rotate, and to move forward.

So the bottom of the larynx is the cricoid ring, the front and sides are composed of the thyroid cartilage, and the back is formed by the arytenoids. Running from the inside of the thyroid notch back to the arytenoids are the two vocal folds. Just behind the thyroid notch, the vocal folds are attached to each other. As they move back toward the arytenoids, they quickly separate into two independent folds, each of which is attached to its own arytenoid cartilage. When the arytenoids are apart, the vocal folds look like a V. When the arytenoids are together, the vocal folds look like two I's side by side (figure 4-5).

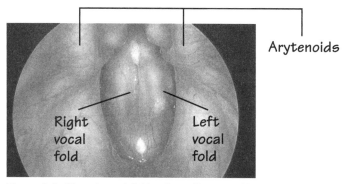

Figure 4-5: Closed vocal folds photo (Courtesy Kay Pentax)

The muscles that control your arytenoids are the primary ones that determine your degree of vocal fold closure. When the vocal folds are brought together and air is exhaled through them, the vocal folds vibrate and voice occurs (this process of valving air with the vocal folds is called *phonation*). The arytenoids can bring the vocal folds together a little bit to give you a very soft sound. They can bring the vocal folds together a perfect amount to give you a nice, warm voice. They can also bring the vocal folds together very tightly, leading to a pressed sound.

Sometimes, they bring the vocal folds together so much that you all of a sudden have a sphincter in there, which is what happens when you swallow. The primary biological function of the vocal folds is to protect the airway. As you breathe, the vocal folds are open, allowing air to pass freely between them without causing them to vibrate. If a foreign body passes by the vocal folds while you breathe in, the vocal folds reflexively come together and clamp shut in an effort to prevent the foreign body from entering your airway. Often, a cough will follow to expel any unwanted objects. The two vocal folds also come together in a closed position when you swallow, clear your throat, talk, sing, bear down, and hold your breath while keeping your mouth open. Whenever you need to close your airway, the vocal folds close.

The muscles that control the vocal folds are quite variable and have a wide breadth of utility. We can learn to control them to a surprising degree.

True or False Vocal Folds?

Interestingly, there are also folds of tissue located just above the true vocal folds that are called the *false vocal folds*—also known as *ventricular folds* (figure 4-6). These folds can come together as well and do so each time you swallow as an extra layer of protec-

tion for your airway. They also usually come together when you grunt, strain, bear down, or hold your breath. For speech and singing, we try to keep our false vocal folds relatively inactive or open.

Incidentally, the false vocal folds often "take over" as the primary source of vibration for voice should the true vocal folds

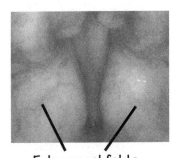

False vocal folds

Figure 4-6: False vocal folds
(Courtesy Kay Pentax)

become severely damaged. False vocal fold vibration is usually low, gruff, and effortful. Louis Armstrong probably achieved his distinctive singing style by using false vocal fold vibration.

The Ceiling of the Larynx

The *hyoid* (HIGH-oid) *bone* is a horseshoe-shaped bone located above, and parallel to, the thyroid cartilage (figure 4-7). Muscles coming up from the top rim of the thyroid cartilage insert into the bottom of the hyoid bone. Muscles of the tongue insert into the top of the hyoid bone. The hyoid bone is the only bone in the larynx. It is also distinctive in that it is the only bone in the body that is suspended between muscles.

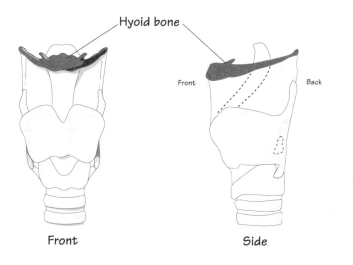

Figure 4-7: Hyoid bone

The *epiglottis* is a leaf-shaped piece of cartilage (figure 4-8). The "stem" inserts into the base of the tongue. The "leaf" curls up and out of the way when we talk, sing, and breathe. When we

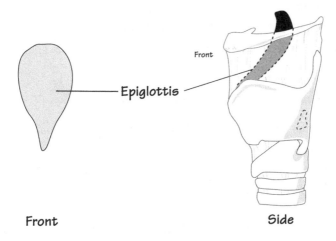

Front   **Side**

Figure 4-8: Epiglottis

swallow, the epiglottis uncurls and covers the top of the larynx. Whatever is being swallowed slides over the top of the epiglottis and into the esophagus (food tube).

Exercises to Explore the Vocal Cords

Finding Your Larynx

To get a feel for where your vocal folds are, put your fingers on your Adam's apple (thyroid lamina) and swallow (figure 4-9). Notice it move up and down. Now, take a deep breath and hold your breath, bearing down, while keeping your mouth open. Your vocal folds are now completely closed. Now, let your breath out. Do you notice a

Figure 4-9: Feeling the larynx

little *click* sound at the beginning? If so, that is the sound of your vocal folds blowing apart. Keeping your fingers on the larynx, say *ah* for five seconds and feel for vibration. Repeat this sound several times in a row.

Feeling Vocal Fold Vibration

Place your fingers on either side of your thyroid lamina. Say *sss-zzz-sss-zzz*. In other words, sound like a snake, then a bee. Feel the vibration of your vocal folds during the bee, *zzz*, and an absence of vibration during the snake, *sss*.

Controlling Vocal Fold Closure

See if you can imagine your vocal folds coming together and apart while you make easy grunting noises (preferably in private). Just before you grunt, your true vocal folds and your false vocal folds are together. Some people can feel this as a slight constriction. The constriction is released as air puffs out.

Understanding the Ups and Downs of Your Larynx

With your finger on your Adam's apple, yawn and feel it go down. Swallow and feel it go up. Can you voluntarily move your larynx up and down?

Quick Notes
- There are two vocal folds.
- They are attached to each other in the front.
- Each one attaches to an arytenoid in the back.
- Arytenoids move the vocal folds together and apart.
- When the arytenoids are touching, the vocal folds are touching.
- When air rushes between vocal folds, vibration occurs.
- Vibration is the result of the vocal folds peeling away from each other, then being sucked back together very quickly.
- The arytenoids stay together to promote vocal fold vibration and move apart to stop vibration.
- When the vocal folds vibrate, they valve the air which in turn produces sound.

Frequently Asked Questions about Vocal Cords

Q: *What happens to my vocal folds as I get older?*

A: The answer to this question is dependent on your general health and your gender. In general, women's vocal folds tend to become slightly larger with age and their voices subsequently become a bit lower in pitch. Men's vocal folds, on the other hand, can become slightly smaller, thereby causing their vocal pitch to be slightly higher. For both men and women, it appears that a lifetime of good physical exercise and balanced nutrition can contribute to a healthy sounding voice in our senior years. As with most muscles, the strength of the vocal fold muscles is affected by the "use it or lose it" phenomenon. Many neurological diseases (e.g., Parkinson's disease, essential tremor, ALS, myasthenia gravis) can also change the shape and/or function of the vocal folds.

Q: *My uncle had heart surgery a year ago. Right after surgery, his voice was hoarse and weak. A year later, his voice is not as hoarse, but he can't project his voice and he becomes tired after talking for over twenty minutes. What happened?*

A: If he hasn't seen an ENT physician already, it would be a good idea for him to get his vocal folds evaluated by one. It is possible that the *recurrent laryngeal nerve* was compromised during surgery, thereby causing one arytenoid to be weakened or paralyzed. Remember that the vocal cords are attached at the back to the arytenoids; the recurrent laryngeal nerve is what makes their opening and closing movement possible. When this nerve becomes damaged, the corresponding arytenoid and vocal cord becomes stuck in one position. If the arytenoid is paralyzed in the closed position, voice quality will be nearly normal. This is because the arytenoids and vocal cords

can still come into complete contact. If, however, the arytenoid is paralyzed in an open position, voice quality will be
weak, breathy, and even "fluttery," as the vocal folds will not
come into contact with each other. There are surgeries that
can move a vocal fold that is paralyzed in the open position to
the closed position, which can greatly improve voice quality.
Voice therapy can also improve vocal quality issues resulting
from laryngeal nerve damage.

Q: *Where do nodes grow, and how do you get them?*

A: Nodes, or nodules, occur at the midpoint of the vibrating
vocal folds. They are caused primarily by impact force (the
intensity of the force when the folds come together). The
midpoint is the area of greatest impact force. Nodules generally start out as edema (swelling), which occurs if the impact
force to the folds is more traumatic than they can handle.
If this swelling has a chance to heal, nodules will not form.
If, however, the impact force continues, the vocal fold tissue can be damaged, and thready fibers (which are collagen, or similar to it) can accumulate in a gelatinous layer of
the vocal folds. These fibers constitute nodules. Factors that
lower the tolerance of the vocal folds to impact force include
dehydration, irritation (due to upper-respiratory infection
or laryngopharyngeal reflux), as well as genetic predisposition. More detail is provided in chapter 10.

5

Tweaking the Filter Settings: Vocal Resonance

For our purposes, *resonance* refers to a vocal sound that is full and rich. All voices have some degree of resonance, but have you noticed that some voices are much more resonant than others? A full, warm voice tends to hold high appeal in our society and is a common goal for many of our clients. This is because a resonant voice not only sounds attrac-

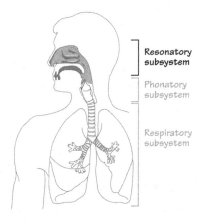

Resonatory subsystem

Phonatory subsystem

Respiratory subsystem

tive but is usually produced with a relaxed larynx, throat, and mouth. Using resonance helps people, with or without vocal injuries, improve their vocal access, comfort, and quality.

One client, a high school French teacher, arrived for a voice evaluation with sig-

nificant loss of vocal resonance. She complained that her voice had become increasingly weak and hoarse over the past several years. Evaluation revealed that her voice was breathy, reedy, thin, and lacking in resonance. She explained that her voice had not changed much since she came to the United States from France at the age of twelve. She did not learn English quickly, and she felt that her lack of confidence about the language caused her voice to stay in an "uncertain" place for these many years. During the one session in which she learned to produce voice with a strong, forward resonance, she was astounded. She had never experienced her full voice before, and its ease and power amazed her. After a course of voice therapy, she was able to lecture with vocal stability and strength, eliminate her weekly episodes of voice loss, and even sing French folk songs from her youth to her classes.

What our client learned, and what you will learn, too, is that voice quality can be improved simply by changing the shape of your throat and mouth.

The Vocal Tract

The vocal tract (throat, mouth, and nose) filters the sound created by vocal fold vibration. It is the combination of vocal fold vibration and the vocal tract that gives you your unique voice quality, or voiceprint. The concept of filtering a sound is familiar to most of us. A lot of stereos have buttons you can push to select a particular sound, such as jazz and rock. Pressing these buttons changes the quality of the music a bit; they might make the bass sound stronger or make the music sound mellower. They filter the sound by enhancing certain tones and damping down others. These are fancy electronic filters, but sound filters come in all shapes and sizes. Take, for example, a paper towel tube as a filter. If you talk through the tube, your voice sounds different because the tube filters the sound. The vocal tract is basically a movable, dynamic tube/filter. The size and shape of the vocal tract determine, in part, the sound of the voice.

When you blow into the mouthpiece of a trumpet without the bell attached, you create a buzzy, unfocused sound. With the bell attached, the sound becomes full, rich, and brassy. Similarly, if you could vibrate a set of vocal cords outside the body, the resultant sound would bear no relation to voice. It is the coupling of vocal fold vibration with the vocal tract that determines voice quality.

The vocal tract is made up of many muscles that we call "who knew?" muscles. Who knew that they were there? Who knew that we could control them, and who knew that we could have tension in them?

We begin with our first series of "who knew?" muscles in the throat. The back of the throat is actually a tube of muscles called the *pharynx*. When we swallow, that tube constricts and squeezes the food down into the esophagus. A lot of us maintain some degree of squeezing and constriction of those muscles all the time. This interferes with voice. We want the tube to have its naturally big diameter, especially at the part that "rounds the bend" from the throat to the mouth. It should be like a drinking straw that has a flexible bend in it, as opposed to a straight drinking straw that closes up when it bends.

The rest of the vocal tract is made up of the articulators and the nose. The *articulators* are the tongue, lower jaw, teeth, lips, roof of the mouth (the hard palate and soft palate), and gum ridge (also called the *alveolar arch*). We change the shape of the vocal tract all the time without thinking about it. Depending on how we shape those muscles, we get totally different sounds. Experiment with your own vocal tract. Hold out the sound *eee*, for example, as in the word "feel." Notice that your tongue is very high in your mouth. Now hold out the sound *ah* as in "father." Notice that your tongue is relatively low in your mouth. Next go back and forth, *eee, ah, eee, ah, eee, ah*, without moving your jaw. Your tongue moves up, down, up, down, up, down (figure 5-1). The only difference between those sounds is placement of your tongue in your mouth, which changes the shape of the vocal tract.

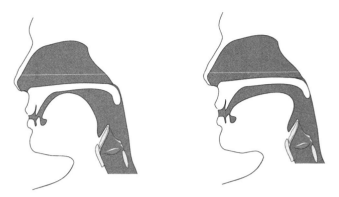

Figure 5-1: Side view of mouth for the vowel *eee* (left) and *ah* (right)

Remember that if you make a sound through a tube, the sound that comes out the other end depends on the shape of the tube. In general we want the vocal tract to be big (or at least not made smaller due to tension), and we want to direct the voice to the front of the vocal tract. We don't want it to get lost anywhere. When people talk about feeling like their voice is "stuck in their throat," or like they "talk from their throat," it's usually because the vocal tract is tight in the throat or the tongue is pulled back and the sound cannot make it all the way out.

Vocal Tract Tour

Let's take a closer look at the vocal tract in the human body. Understanding this area helps you maximize your voice. The vocal tract has several degrees of freedom, meaning that it can be controlled and reshaped with surprising precision and flexibility.

Ground Floor

We'll start our exploration at the bottom of the vocal tract, the larynx. The larynx (which houses the vocal folds) is capable of moving up and down in the neck. Put your fingers on your larynx (Adam's apple) and swallow. You will feel the larynx move up and back down. Keep your fingers there and yawn. You'll feel your larynx move down. If your larynx moves up, all other things being equal, the vocal tract becomes shorter because you are essentially raising the floor. A high larynx can result in a tinny or shrill speaking-voice quality. The larynx can also be lowered, which, with all else being equal, lengthens the vocal tract. Lengthening the vocal tract will usually allow a warmer sound, but you don't want to keep the larynx lowered all the time. We want the larynx to move freely in speech without being tethered to either extreme.

Going Up

As we venture upward from the vocal cords, we are now traveling through the pharynx. The pharynx is a tube made entirely of muscle. When these muscles contract, they constrict the vocal tract. This occurs naturally in swallowing. Some of us unwittingly keep a little of the swallowing tension in the throat when we talk. When you relax and widen the pharynx, it makes the vocal tract larger, which makes the voice more resonant.

Next Stop, the Tongue

Remember that the base of the tongue actually inserts into the top of the larynx at the hyoid bone. From the hyoid bone, it runs upward to form the floor of the vocal tract. The tongue muscles are some of the strongest and fastest muscles in the body. As the tongue moves into the many various positions required for forming vowels and consonants, it is constantly changing the shape of the vocal tract.

Rounding the Bend: The Nasality Muscle

Right above the tongue, at the back of the roof of your mouth, you will find the soft palate (also known as the *velum* or *velar port*). If you run your tongue along the roof of your mouth from front to back, you will feel the palate go from hard (bone) to soft (muscle) about three-quarters of the way back. You can actually see your soft palate by opening your mouth very widely and

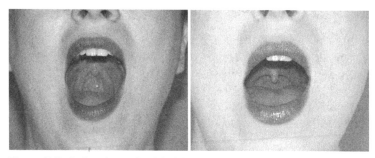

Figure 5-2: Soft palate raised (left) and lowered (right)

looking back as far as you can (figure 5-2). You will see something that looks like a punching bag hanging down right behind the roof of your mouth. This is called your *uvula* (YOU-view-la) and is part of your soft palate.

The soft palate is like a door that separates the mouth and nose—almost like an attic door that opens by being pulled down from the ceiling. It can lift and seal off the doorway between the mouth and nose, or it can open downward and connect them (figure 5-3).

This is an important movable part of the vocal tract because the space is changed appreciably depending on whether the palate is opened (dropped) or closed (raised). If it is open, your vocal tract tube includes your nose, and that means that air is getting into the nose during speech. This results in a nasal sound.

For regular speech, the soft palate opens and closes frequently, allowing us to make the nasal and nonnasal sounds as needed.

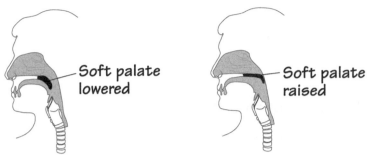

Figure 5-3: Side view of soft palate in mouth

In English, there are only three sounds that require strong nasal resonance, or air in the nose. They are *m*, *n*, and *ng*. You can feel the effect of this nasal resonance by holding your nose and trying to make one of those sounds. You can't do it (as if you had a "cold id your dose"), because the air has to come through the nose. If the soft palate is always open, then the sound that we produce is probably excessively nasal.

Last Stop: The Lips

Finishing up our vocal tract tour, let's go to the very front: the lips. If you move your lips forward (as for a kiss or as in the sound *ooo*), you lengthen the vocal tract (figure 5-4). And, again, with a lengthened vocal tract, your voice is more likely to sound lower and warm. The lips can also spread apart (as in a smile or the sound *eee*). When the lips spread in that way, the vocal tract is effectively shortened (figure 5-5).

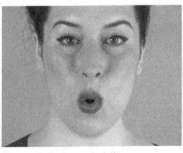

Figure 5-4: Rounded lips   Figure 5-5: Spread lips

Holding a steady sound, move between the sounds *ooo* (as in "boo") and *eee* (as in "bee"). Can you hear that the pitch seems to change?

How *Not* to Have a Resonant Voice

Many people enter into voice training with a desire to make their speaking voices lower, deeper, or richer because they feel that their voices sound too high. And, usually, the pitch of the voice itself is not too high (as dictated by the number of times per second that the vocal folds vibrate), but rather the vocal tract is so constricted that it is artificially made smaller, thereby amplifying the higher overtones and giving the *illusion* of a higher pitch. So people who are trying to lower their voices can end up developing an injury because they are speaking at a pitch that is unnaturally low. The key is opening the vocal tract and adding resonance and richness that way.

You may recognize some of the following ways that people inadvertently shorten the vocal tract. One way is to raise the larynx by misaligning the head. There is a ligament that runs from the larynx to the bone behind your ear. So if you jut your chin forward or upward, the larynx is yanked up by this ligament. Another way to shorten the vocal tract is to smile. A lot of people tend to keep their "smile" muscles slightly contracted on a regular basis. This shortens the vocal tract and gives the speaking voice a higher and potentially more "pinched" quality. A third common way to shorten the vocal tract is through jaw tension. Because the lower jaw moves the underside of the vocal tract, keeping the jaw tight makes the vocal tract smaller.

Therefore, to create the rich, warm, resonant voice that you want, maintain an aligned head, relaxed jaw and facial muscles, open vocal tract, and free tongue.

Using the Vocal Tract to Change Vocal Loudness

Loudness is often one of the most salient characteristics perceived about a voice. You have probably heard people say, "Whew, that guy was a loud talker," or "She mumbled; I could barely hear her." Vocal loudness that is different than what is expected calls attention to itself.

All three of the subsystems of speech influence loudness. First, all other things being equal, the more air pressure you have underneath your vocal cords to set them into vibration, the louder you will be. The amount of air we use is probably the primary way in which we become louder and softer.

Second, if the vocal folds are not quite touching each other, if they are held apart and are still maintaining a bit of a V shape, then the loudness will decrease. If the vocal folds are fully in contact with each other while they vibrate, then the voice is likely to be louder. However, if the vocal folds are brought together too tightly, they can't vibrate well, and the voice becomes tight and less loud.

Last, the vocal tract also influences loudness. If the pharynx is tight or the tongue is bunched up in the back of the mouth during speech, this tension acts like a mute on the end of a trumpet. It will "trap" the sound and prevent it from projecting forward. Effective releasing and opening of the vocal tract during speech can naturally boost vocal volume. This is a safe and effective way to increase vocal volume without causing vocal fold injury because it doesn't necessarily increase the amount of impact force between your vocal cords. What it does change is how well your voice carries from your mouth to your listener. In fact, vocal tract shaping is one of the most important aspects of vocal efficiency training. Done correctly, it can lengthen the amount of time you are able to speak without becoming hoarse or vocally fatigued.

Finding the vocal tract shape that optimally amplifies your own voice boosts loudness dramatically and is the key to resonance.

Vocal Placement: What Is It and Why Is It Important?

Vocal placement is a term used commonly in both speech and singing training. *Placement*, in this context, refers to the place in the vocal tract where sound is "felt" through vibration. For most speech training, as well as voice rehabilitation, a forward placement of the voice is encouraged because it usually entails healthy vocal cord movement. Forward placement produces a feeling of vibration in the bone above your upper lip, the bone in which your top front four teeth are inserted. The sections below describe how to achieve that kind of resonance.

Finding Your Resonant, Strong Voice

We think Kristin Linklater's *Freeing the Natural Voice* is a perfect book title because it describes a key goal of most voice training. The goal here is not to teach you an artificial voice but rather to undo habituated tensions in the vocal mechanism. In short, we want to help you find your natural voice—your most efficient voice, the one that you are designed to use. Our belief is that, barring vocal injury, any voice that is not resonant and strong most likely sounds the way it does because of some type of tension in the vocal tract.

We remind you again of the relevance of habit. Much of the habituated tension to which we refer is in the "who knew?" muscle groups. Awareness always precedes change. So as we move through these exercises, make friends with your vocal tract and become *aware* of the muscles that we describe in this section.

Here is one final anecdote from our clinical experience to motivate you. A high-level corporate sales executive came for voice training because he had stage fright when he presented. His voice, unbeknownst to him, was throaty, gravelly, and tight. When he learned to create voice with a forward resonance, many things shifted for him. He felt more confident (his stage fright vanished), was more readily understood by his clients, and enjoyed his work more. (We know this sounds like hyperbole, but we swear it isn't!)

14 Steps to Build Your Resonant Voice

The following progression is hierarchical (it builds on itself). We recommend that you master each step before moving on to the next. It is preferable, for instance, to spend your entire practice session really mastering the early steps rather than whipping through the whole progression but not really hitting the target.

Throughout the exercises, you are aiming for a feeling, not a sound. This is an unfamiliar concept for some people. While we are providing models for you to hear and essentially mimic, the ultimate goal is for you to acquaint yourself with the *feeling* of making sound in this way. What we hear can be unreliable. What we feel is reliable and accurate. Go for the feel.

1. Anchoring

Come to the resting position described in chapter 2, with your head balanced on top of your body, chin level, lips gently touching, jaw relaxed so there is space between your upper and lower back teeth, and the back of the tongue low and flat like a rug

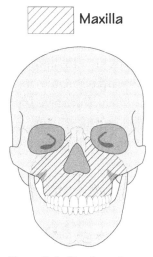

Maxilla

Figure 5-6: The "sweet spot" for voice

on the floor of the mouth. Take a moment to breathe, and invite your neck and throat muscles to relax. Take a little breath in and, as if you are agreeing with something, say *mm-hmm*. Repeat. Now bring your awareness to the bone in which your four upper front teeth are inserted—the bone between your nose and your upper lip (figure 5-6).

Keep that resting position (check the back of the tongue—it's wily!) and again repeat *mm-hmm* and aim to feel a vibration in that bone, which is called the *maxilla*, or upper jawbone. This *mm-hmm* sound, vibrating fully in the maxilla, is your anchor.

2. Arcing

Let's take this concept and apply it to a different sound. Keeping the same vibration in that bone above your upper lip, take a breath and instead of saying *mm-hmm*, say *hmm* as though pondering something. There is an arc to the sound: the pitch starts higher and drops a bit, like shooting a basketball into the hoop. As in the previous exercise, the intention is to feel vibration in the bone above the upper lip. You may feel vibration in your upper lip; that's good too.

If you don't feel that vibration, check to make sure that your tongue is low in the back (though not pressed down). Usually a high, tense tongue in the back is what interferes with the vibration. If your tongue is low and you still don't feel a vibration, make sure that you have enough breath. If your tongue is low and you have enough breath and you still don't feel a vibration, see if you're using too much breath. If that doesn't work, check and make sure that your jaw is released. If that still doesn't work, see if your pitch has strayed from your natural speaking pitch (most people tend to let the pitch drop).

If all of these factors are in place, check the X factor. By that we mean to "think your voice forward." The intention is to place the voice in the front of the face and feel the vibration in this bone above the upper lip. So once again, with your head aligned, jaw dropped, tongue flat, and neck long, take a breath and arc the sound *hmm*. Practice with the CD until you feel this vibration.

3. Increasing Forward Vibrations

Take in a little belly breath, check your alignment, and sustain *mmm* at a comfortable pitch. Make sure that you can feel the vibration in the maxilla and that you are arcing your sound.

Next, while you sustain that tone, gently allow your jaw to open and close and allow your tongue to explore different positions inside your mouth. Observe what happens to the intensity of the vibration that you feel in the front of the face. Notice which mouth position increases the intensity of vibration. Be sure to keep your vocal effort consistent. If you are having trouble feeling the vibration, try a slightly higher pitch.

Mental requests to your body are more effective if made simple and direct. Focus on what you want to do (e.g., feel the vibration in your maxilla) rather than "getting it right." Check your mental requests while doing resonance exercises.

4. Finding Forward Vowels

Take in a little breath and begin with your steady *mmm* sound, feeling the vibration in the bone above your lip. Repeat your anchor (*mm-hmm*) and make sure the vibration is as strong here as it is in the anchor. Now you are going to open up to the sound *mum*. And you will do that on one pitch several times in a row like this:

mmm-mum, mum, mum, mum

Listen to the CD for an example. Notice that as you open up your lips for the *uh* part of the sound *mum*, you may no longer feel the vibration in your maxilla. When you open up your lips for the *uh*, you have less sensory information in the front of your face to go by, but you will eventually still feel a slight vibration there during the *uh*. Your goal is to sustain forward placement through the vowel so that you seamlessly move from the *m* at the beginning of the word to the *m* at the end of the word.

Try with the following sequences:

mmm-mim, mim, mim, mim
mmm-mohm, mohm, mohm, mohm
mmm-moom, moom, moom, moom
mmm-mam, mam, mam, mam
mmm-maim, maim, maim, maim
mmm-mem, mem, mem, mem
mmm-mom, mom, mom, mom

> Make a mental request to yourself to *do* something rather than to *try* to do something.

On each *m* sound, feel the vibration strongly. Hold out the *m* until you can really tell whether you feel it, then move on through the sequence.

5. Feeling *N*

Say *nn-hnn,* which is the same as saying *mm-hmm,* but with an *n* rather than an *m* sound. With your tongue tip *very lightly* touching the front of the palate, say *nn-hnn* and feel the vibration in that same bone. Repeat exercises 1–4 using *n* instead of *m*.

In golf, players are instructed to hold a single thought in their minds as they swing. This is referred to as the "swing thought." The swing thought for the remainder of these exercises is to concentrate on feeling vibration in your maxilla. That is the goal. It is easy to go through the motions in exercises as apparently simple as the ones presented here. When you are intentionally focused and aware and present, these exercises become remarkably complex. So hold in your consciousness the feeling of that vibration in your maxilla as you move through the remainder of the progression. You can only achieve this goal by being focused on the present moment.

6. Forward Focus: One Syllable I

Say the following one-syllable words while maintaining a feeling of forward vibration.

me	new
moo	neigh
my	no
may	naw
maw	

7. Forward Focus: One Syllable II

Move to one-syllable words that begin or end with an *m* or *n*. The swing thought remains to focus on feeling vibration on the *m* or *n*, at the beginning or the end of the word. Return to the anchor to feel the vibration in your maxilla. Replicate this vibration when you say the *m* and *n* sounds in these words.

mom	mean
men	mine
man	moo
line	vine
noon	main
moon	mime

8. Forward Focus: Two Syllables

Apply the same forward placement to two-syllable words and word combinations.

many	mailman
Molly	movement
namely	migraine
no one	young man
monkey	wowee
marine	nine men
minute	win one
Nemo	lemon
mermaid	movie
merman	narrow
moaning	maintain
measure	women
ninety	more wine

9. Forward Focus: Three and Four Syllables

Now that you have the hang of it, try three- and four-syllable words and phrases.

nine million	medieval
many mums	Melanie
marshmallow	musical
mail my memo	one million
my lawn mower	magazine
win nine million	more money
lemon lamb	medium

Practice building up:

No
No one
No one knew
No one knew my name
No one knew my name in Maine
No one knew my name in Maine in May

Are you in alignment? If not, can you change your position so that you are?

10. Forward Focus: Phrases

You may have noticed that it is easier to train forward vibration if you stay on one note. When you do this, you may initially sound like a robot. Obviously, we don't speak that way, so it is important to move into natural-sounding speech as soon as possible. However, for the purpose of learning, we are going to start by chanting the following phrases, and then we will move through the same phrases again with natural-sounding inflection.

The first time you read through the following phrases, sustain the sound *m* or *n* to train the forward vibration. Then chant the entire phrase while maintaining that vibration.

The second time through, simply say the phrase with normal inflection. The main thought is to focus on feeling the vibration on the maxilla with every *m* or *n* sound. That is the only thought that needs to be in your mind. In the beginning, you will need to sustain the *m* and *n* sounds longer than normal in order to feel them. Eventually, you will be able to feel the vibration more quickly and will not need to sustain the sound as long. Listen to the CD for an example.

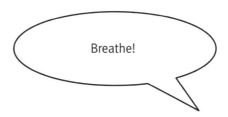

My momma made lemon jam
Mary moved to Memphis
Mark and Mona were mad at me
Marge made a mountain of money in Nebraska

Meet me in my room tomorrow at noon

When I came home, my mom made me move my many marbles

Nana munches on lemon melons

I missed Mike at the movie this morning

My maid is messy

Madge loves lemon meringue pies

Come home with me to Memphis this summer

Meg's mother is monotonous

Michelle's market sells lemon, melon, jam, and moonshine

Mayor Mike roamed around the mall

Morton's team will meet Megan's team on Monday

Morning sun in the morning in Maine

11. Forward Focus: Paragraph

Speak the following paragraph while keeping forward vibration:

Many times a year Mary's mom makes muffins.
These muffins tend to be mushy and, therefore,
pretty messy. You need a napkin when you eat
them. Muffins are made with many ingredients
including milk, sugar, and butter. When you buy
the milk, make sure it does not smell sour.

12. Forward Focus: Conversation I

Start with the word "hum." When saying "hum," the *h* gets your air moving, the *uh* lowers your tongue, and the *mmm* brings your voice forward to your maxilla. Be sure to arc your sound.

Hum
HummmOne
HummmOneTwo
HummmOneTwoThree
HummmOneTwoThreeFour
HummmOneTwoThreeFourFive

Motor learning requires repetition.
Remember the importance of practice.

Next, say a short phrase directly after saying "hum," keeping the feeling of forward vibration throughout. For example, "*Hummm* my sweater is brown." As you say "hum," keep saying that *m* until you feel the vibration in the maxilla. Do not move into the phrase until you feel that sensation. The idea is that the *m* in "hum" places the voice forward, and then the phrase that you say afterward follows along in its wake, like a water skier being pulled behind a motor boat. Once you can do five in a row while maintaining the forward vibration, move on to the next step.

13. Forward Focus: Conversation II

As in exercise 12, begin with "hum," but follow it with a full sentence. Take a breath and say the same sentence again without the "hum." For example, "*Hummm* the walls are made of wood"—breathe in—"The walls are made of wood." The second sentence has the same degree of forward resonance as the sentence with the "hum." Once you can do five in a row on target, move on.

14. Forward Focus: Conversation III

Make up short phrases without the "hum" and place them in the front of your face. It is helpful to return to the anchor (*mm-hmm* from exercise 1) throughout this exercise. This reminds you of what the target is. Most people are used to speaking with virtually no vibration in the front of the face at all, so any vibration can feel like the target. This is not the case. The goal is the *most* possible vibration with no effort. On an arbitrary 10-point scale of vibration, your anchor (the *mm-hmm* sound) will produce a 10—the most vibration you can feel on any particular day at any particular moment. Your 10 might shift due to time of day, amount of rest, and so on. You want to always be working with the most possible vibration. As you go through the exercises, insert the anchor every few phrases to remind yourself of your target.

Troubleshooting Tips

If you can't feel any vibration, try the following suggestions.

Tongue Tension

The number one culprit for blocking the vibration is a high, tense back of the tongue. Since there are other negative effects of tongue tension on the voice, this is the first thing to check. If the back of the tongue is overly tense (and, therefore, raised), it literally blocks the passage for the air (see figures 5-7 and 5-8).

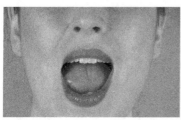 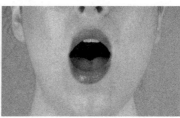

Figure 5-7: High back of tongue   Figure 5-8: Lowered tongue

The way you make the maxilla vibrate is by opening the voice channel and directing the vibrating column of air valved by the vocal folds to hit the bone. If there is an obstruction in that passageway, it is not possible to create that vibration.

Jaw Tension

For the same reasons given above, if you are not feeling the desired vibration, check how widely you are opening your jaw while keeping your lips together. Try making the space between your upper and lower teeth bigger, wide enough to put your tongue between your upper and lower molars. You could also try exaggerated chewing. Really drop your jaw while keeping your lips together, as though you had a large piece of bubble gum inside your mouth, and feel the vibration maximized by that large mouth opening.

Breath

You need to have enough breath to make the vibration. And here's the tricky part: you can also have too much breath. The goal is to have the right amount of breath for the task, and more is definitely not always better.

Pitch

Sometimes the effort of trying to succeed at the exercise can cause an unnaturally low pitch. Return to the pitch used in the *mm-hmm* anchor.

Intention

Very often what is missing is the X factor of simply thinking the sound forward. This can correlate to a feeling of sending your voice out of you.

Frequently Asked Questions about Resonance

Q: *I don't feel my maxilla vibrate when I talk in everyday life. Am I doing something wrong?*

A: Not feeling forward vibration when you are speaking could possibly indicate that you are missing something. It is always good to go back to your anchor. Make sure that your anchor is reflecting a strong vibration that is unmistakably forward. Then go through exercises throughout the hierarchy to build your forward voice up to conversation.

Not perceiving vibration during speech could also be simply a matter of attention. Once you start speaking, your mental resources are more spread out as you formulate language and attend to your listener. The amount of attention that you are able to pay to feeling that forward vibration might be the only thing that is missing.

Q: *I feel like I am talking really loud. Am I?*

A: It is often easier for people to master these techniques at a slightly louder level than they would normally use to speak. In some ways this is good. The qualities that create a strong voice—the forward resonance and open vocal tract, not to mention the increased breath support required for the forward resonance—lead to louder speech than people tend to use habitually. So you may be speaking louder, and our recommendation is to go ahead and practice that way until you have the techniques down, and then work on decreasing the volume. Otherwise, you might get quiet either by decreasing your breath support and putting the focus of your voice in your throat or by getting breathy (whispery tone). Usually, those are not recommended. So unless you are straining, don't be concerned about the volume, and remember what you are currently doing when you actually need to be loud!

It is also possible that you are not especially loud but simply sound that way to yourself because of the resonance. We hear other people through air conduction (outside-in), but we hear ourselves through bone conduction (inside-out). By increasing the vibration in the bones of your skull, you could sound louder to yourself.

Q: *Do I sound funny?*

A: Most likely, yes. In the beginning. Keep in mind that the way we sound to ourselves is often quite different from how we sound to others. The best way to determine what you sound like is to record yourself while achieving forward resonance, and then play it back. You may have habituated your voice out of a desire to sound a particular way. You might be interested to know what you sound like when "freeing" your natural voice. You can then decide if this is funny or if this is pleasant.

Also, it is common to inadvertently sound like a robot in the beginning stages of this work. If that is so, make your inflection as natural as possible. You can use even more pitch variety with an open system than with a constricted one. With time, the natural voice that you are liberating will sound . . . more natural.

Q: *You say that my tongue should be low, but I feel it moving when I talk. Am I doing it wrong?*

A: No. Laying your tongue flat on the floor of your mouth is what you are shooting for when you are not using it to make speech. When you talk, however, the tongue moves all over the place. It moves up, down, sideways, forward, and back. It is impossible to speak without the tongue moving. (Some voice training systems—the Estill Voice Training System, for example—train the use of a raised tongue during some styles of singing and possibly speech.) That being said, the base of the tongue (where it rounds the bend and goes down the throat) is the area in question. The goal is to release tension there. And for most of us, that involves releasing the tongue down and back. It is as though the very back of the mouth is always saying *ah* no matter what the rest of the tongue is doing.

Q: *My voice feels tired at the end of my exercises. Am I doing something wrong?*

A: It depends on what kind of tired you feel. Using the muscles in a new way could result in some fatigue. This is OK. Or you could be straining unnecessary muscles in your well-intentioned attempt to manipulate the ones in question. If it results in a scratchy, coughlike feeling low in the throat, this is not good. Keep in mind that you probably haven't ever thought about your vocal tract in this way before. So when you bring your attention, for example, to your pharynx, you might be inadvertently tensing those muscles (or neighboring ones) to assure yourself that you are, indeed, thinking about the pharynx. As you practice and are able to relax and manipulate the vocal tract, you will be able to go through these exercises without any fatigue.

Q: *I'm working with the CD, but I don't sound like you and, in fact, I don't sound right at all. What should I do?*

A: Remember that the goal here is to learn how to attend to your voice and to feel it. The feel of forward vibration is primary, and the sound is secondary. Also, the goal isn't to end up sounding like the CD but rather to sound like you without any extraneous tension. *Vive la différence!*

Q: *I just can't tell if I am doing it right. Can you help me?*

A: Do you feel the vibration? If yes, you are on the right track. If you don't, release frustration and remember that people rarely hit targets the first time through. Check to make sure you are truly attending to the specific goal of feeling forward vibration. Then, move through the troubleshooting section of this chapter and give your body specific commands. The more specific you are, the more likely it is to obey. If you give your body a command like, "I want to sound better and I want to get it right" it doesn't know how to do that. If you give your body a command like, "Bring my head into alignment and relax the tongue," it will understand and cooperate. Hang in there for a few weeks; consistent practice will lead to change.

Q: *I don't feel vibration on the anchor no matter what I do. Am I doing it wrong?*

A: You might be producing the vibration but unable to feel it. Place your fingertips very lightly on the part of your face above the upper lip (don't press). Say the anchor and see if you feel the vibration in your fingertips. Many people are so unaccustomed to this type of subtle kinesthetic awareness that it takes time to learn to feel it from the inside. If you feel the vibration in your fingertips, work from there to learn to identify the feeling from the inside.

6

Creating Music and Flow: Easy Onset, Linking, and Emphasis

Did you know that using inflection when you talk can reduce vocal fatigue? By varying the way you emphasize words, you can reduce the chance of overusing laryngeal muscles. Another way to reduce vocal strain is to gently pronounce vowel sounds when they occur at the beginning of a word. Mastering these techniques will reduce the likelihood of vocal injury and help your speech sound melodious, clear, and interesting.

Easy Onset and Linking

The primary goal of easy onset and linking is to minimize hard glottal attacks, or slamming together of the vocal folds, in speech. Hard glottal attacks occur when the vocal folds (and usually the false vocal folds) compress, then abruptly release. This can cause more impact force between the vocal folds than is healthy; as we will discuss in chapter 10, vocal fold impact force can lead to vocal injury. Also, because we can't breathe through tightly closed vocal folds, each time they slam together we hold our breath for a brief duration. So hard glottal attacks not only create extra impact force for the vocal folds, but they also disrupt the breath stream, making our speech sound choppy. If our goal is to have a sense of easy flow to voicing, we want to eliminate choppiness.

Easy onset applies only to words that begin with a vowel sound. The onset of a vowel sound, or the way we begin that sound, can be achieved three different ways.

1. With a hard glottal attack: the vocal folds compress, then abruptly release to create a sudden and often sharp onset to a vowel.

2. With an aspirate initiation: too much air is allowed to escape before your vocal folds begin to vibrate and make sound. This usually results in an *h* sound.

3. With easy onset: your vocal folds come together without compression, then smoothly begin to vibrate as air is exhaled through them. This is what we are going for.

The best way to learn easy onset is with auditory modeling, following along with track 6 on the CD. In this chapter's exercises, we will practice initiating words in each of the three ways described above. Sometimes it is easier to acquire a new skill by purposefully doing it the undesirable way to heighten awareness.

Linking refers to connecting words together. In the sentence "I am eating an orange an hour," every word starts with a vowel sound. Read that sentence aloud, pronouncing each word separately. Notice how choppy it sounds, and how easy it is to begin each word with a hard glottal attack.

To avoid this, you can link the words together so that the sentence flows like an uninterrupted river of sound. The way to do that is to take the final sound of one word and to use it—like a bridge—to link into the beginning of the next word. To link the words "an orange," you take the *n* from "an" and put it onto the beginning of the word "orange." So it is as though you are saying "anorange." Read through the sentence again, this time linking all the sounds together.

If you say a word pair like "one orange," you take the ending consonant of "one" and put it onto the beginning of "orange," and you say "onenorange." If you say "two oranges," there is no consonant sound at the end of the word "two," but rather a vowel that involves lip rounding. In that case, insert a *w* sound: "twoworanges." If you say "three oranges," with the final sound ending in an *ee* sound, insert a "y" so you say "threeyoranges."

Exercises to Explore Easy Onset and Linking 6

Onset Options

To do this exercise, say each of the words below three times. The first time you say the word, say it with a hard glottal attack. The second time, say the word with an aspirate onset (for example, by placing an obvious *h* sound in front of the word). The third time you say the word, produce the initial vowel sound with easy onset. If you have trouble doing this, start the word with a silent *h*. To achieve easy onset, imagine the sound and airflow beginning at the same time.

eat	ash
am	air
arrow	is
all	Ed
arbor	as
ear	Ike
ought	eyes
art	out
ate	ever
I	also

Let's practice the silent *h*. First, make an *h* sound. Notice that you can hear that sound, and there is a whispering sensation in your throat. To make that sound audible, you constrict your throat muscles. Now let the same amount of air flow out as though you were making an *h*, but don't let yourself hear it. Keep practicing until you are able to send some air out without hearing it at all. This is the silent *h*. It is airflow without constriction.

Practicing Both Techniques

Say the following sentences in your habitual way while noticing your typical onsets for words beginning with a vowel. Then say the sentences a second time, with an effort to use easy onset and linking.

Honesty is always the best policy.
I will always think about you.
Everyone is interested in Eric's opinion.
Ann is older than any of you.
Oh no! I dropped an apple.
Emily exhibited exciting artwork.
Are you and Ann meeting Ira at the movies?
I want to see if we can go tomorrow.
Only a few people were at the store.
Ann expects Alex to investigate our accident.
I'll be going to Annapolis any day now.
I observed interesting animals in Oregon.
Ira is always angry with Ellen.
An ounce of ice cream is all I need.

As you begin to practice, the initial goal is simply for you to notice whether you are linking the words together and beginning with easy onset. Once you are aware of your current tendencies, you can train yourself to use both techniques more consistently.

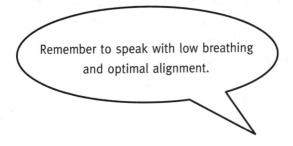

Remember to speak with low breathing and optimal alignment.

Emphasis

Communication is a multifaceted system. We often think of it as simply the language that one uses to convey an idea or a message, but it is much more comprehensive than that. A good deal of what we communicate is through body language, eye contact, posture, and tone of voice. Tone of voice often carries just as much information as language does; in fact, tone of voice can convey your intention even more effectively than the words that you choose. Only 7 percent of our meaning is conveyed through the words we use. Tone of voice conveys a whopping 38 percent of meaning, and body language the remaining 55 percent. A sarcastic declaration such as "That's just great!" makes the relevance of tone clear. Because tone of voice is such an important aspect of communication, our goal is to use vocal tones in a way that encourages an interesting, expressive, and engaging communication style.

When you perceive a speaker as particularly expressive, most likely that speaker has taken advantage of *emphasis* (also known as *intonation* or *prosody*), the stress contrast located within each word and each sentence to make his speech sound interesting to you.

If you find a speaker to be particularly monotonous or droning, most likely the person is not using variation in loudness or pitch in order to bring out key words and the stressed parts of words. Many people produce these contrasting stresses intuitively, while others do not. Once you become aware of how to stress words, you can choose a more expressive and interesting way of speaking. Not only does vocal variety increase communicative effectiveness, but it also engages listeners.

> As you read silently, what kind of pitch variety and emphasis do you "hear"?

Every word in English with more than one syllable contains both stressed and unstressed syllables. This means that one syllable is relatively stronger, or more heavily emphasized, than the other(s). For example, in the word "today" the two syllables are "to" and "day." The second syllable, "day," is the stronger of the two.

Some other words that have a weaker first syllable and a stronger second syllable include "away," "hello," "because," "review," "reduce," and "although." Say them aloud and exaggerate the difference between the weak first syllable and the strong second syllable. Tap your hand on your leg as you speak to feel the "ba-BUM" rhythm of these words.

By contrast, the following words have a relatively stronger first syllable. Say them aloud and notice the contrast between the stronger first syllable and the weak second syllable: "writer," "glasses," "mother," "candle," "wallet," "juggle."

How did you stress the strong syllable? Most likely, it was through one or more of the following techniques: making the pitch higher, making the syllable louder, or by stretching it out. Try it again and see what you notice.

In addition to strong and weak syllables within words, stress is also used within sentences to emphasize the most important words. An aspiring radio broadcaster was seen for coaching because potential employers repeatedly told her that she sounded "unnatural." She could not figure out what this meant or how to change it, and her critics were unable to expound any further on their complaints. It turned out that the problem was related to the words she chose to emphasize when she spoke. Many of us have heard broadcasters with a similar problem—"Tonight *at* seven the president *of* something will speak *to* someone"—in which the stressed words are not the ones that carry the meaning and do not reflect the way we usually speak. The first part of her coaching focused on choosing which words to emphasize in order to make the meaning clearest. She then learned the techniques in this chapter to stress the words she chose, and the result was that she sounded natural because her emphasis supported the meaning of what she was saying.

The most important word ideally sounds different than the rest of the sentence. In many cases there are also secondary and tertiary stresses in a particular sentence, depending on the intention of the speaker. For instance, if you are trying to convince someone that you don't have a problem with Dave, you might say, "I *like* Dave." However, if you are pointing out that it is Dave that you like as opposed to Roger or Sue, you'd say, "I like *Dave*." Just like stressing single syllables, we increase loudness, pitch, and duration to stress words in a sentence. We also have the added options of getting quieter, articulating more clearly, or adding pauses. The human ear is attracted to change—anything that sets a word apart from the rest of the sentence is an option for stress.

Intonation Techniques **7**

Below are sentences you can read aloud to practice common intonation techniques. In each sentence, we have indicated the word to stress by marking it in italics.

Pitch

Read these sentences aloud and stress the italicized word by going *up* in pitch on only that word (then coming back down for the rest of the sentence).

> I *love* going to the movies.
> I *have* to have popcorn at the movies.
> I prefer to watch movies at *home*.
> We *rent* more movies than we buy.

Now practice stressing the italicized words by *lowering* your pitch.

> Do you think *Laura* knows that?
> Laura knows *everything*; be careful.
> That's *why* Laura is a good leader.
> She keeps her eyes and ears *open*.

Loudness

Stress the indicated word by getting *louder* when you say it.

> My car is making a funny *noise*.
> It's a sort of *squeaking* noise.
> The noise happens when I step on the *brakes*.
> Do you think I *need* new brake pads?

Stress the indicated word by getting *softer* when you say it.

James *constantly* drinks coffee.
He is buzzed on caffeine *most* of the time.
Sleeping has become a real problem for James.
Perhaps James should *switch* to decaf.

Rate

Stretch out the stressed word so it takes a *looong* time to say it.

Thank you for the magazine subscription!
I love reading about ways to *simplify* my life.
The problem is finding *time* to read it.
Jay always makes time for *himself*; I admire that.

Enunciation

Overarticulate the consonant and vowel sounds in the italicized word.

Did you see the *sunset* last night?
The colors were really *stunning*.
It's been *years* since I've seen a sunset like that.
I hope *tonight's* sunset will be as good!

Pauses

Emphasize the italicized word by inserting a little *pause* before or after the word (or both).

He *won't* be late this time.
If he's late, I will be *so* mad.
He knows how *important* it is to you—don't worry.
I'm so *happy* he got here early!

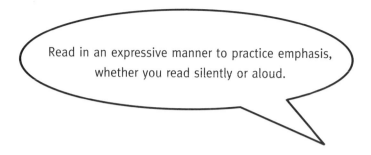

Read in an expressive manner to practice emphasis, whether you read silently or aloud.

Frequently Asked Questions about Easy Onset, Linking, and Emphasis

Q: *Isn't it a good practice to articulate your sounds clearly? I feel like I am mumbling when I link my words together.*

A: This is a very common response. Many people were taught that speaking clearly means separating. each. and. every. word. This is not necessarily the case. While separating words may be a good antidote to mumbling, it may not be the most artful way to articulate clearly. Mumbling means skipping sounds or saying them imprecisely. So if we slur all our words together and skip the final consonants, that would be mumbling. It was in response to that tendency that most people were taught to separate the words. However, in this case, you are actually articulating even more clearly because linking requires you to finish the word before the vowel sound and pronounce the consonant strongly as you link it into the next word. Many people initially feel that connecting the words is slurring or mumbling, but if you listen carefully to yourself and to us on the CD, you will notice that this form of speech requires you to speak more—rather than less—clearly.

Q: *My voice becomes tired, particularly after using my voice recognition software. Will easy onset, linking, and varied emphasis help with this?*

A: Absolutely. Using gentle onsets as well as inflection and variety while dictating helps distribute the "wear and tear" on the vocal folds more evenly than speaking with a flat, unaltered pitch. Varying the length of the vocal folds by changing pitch might help reduce repetitive strain injury–type fatigue. (More information about this topic can be found in chapter 11.)

7

Speech Training: The Lips, the Teeth, the Tip of the Tongue

While this book is predominantly about voice, it is impossible to completely separate voice from speech. *Voice* has to do with the quality of the sound you produce, and *speech* refers to articulating that sound into words. Diction, enunciation, pronunciation, intelligibility, articulation—all refer to speech.

Working on voice can have an impact on your speech. By releasing the jaw and tongue to free your voice, for instance, your speech will be affected because your mouth now has farther to travel to open and close. Likewise, energizing your diction can energize your voice. By training yourself to articulate clearly, you also engage muscles to keep your voice resonant and strong.

Thorough speech training is a broad topic, so we are focusing here on the most common problems and the most powerful techniques—those that can have the quickest impact on a person's speech. We explore several consonant sounds, because they are responsible for most of the crispness and clarity of speech. Strong, energized consonants go a long way to giving the impression of polished speech. We also address vowel sounds, because many people tend to clip or shorten these sounds, which can make speech hard to understand.

Under Pressure

Plosives are a group of six consonant sounds that are made by building up air pressure inside the mouth and then releasing it in a little explosion. Those sounds are *p*, *t*, *k*, *b*, *d*, and *g* (as in "big"). They occur frequently in English, and they provide a strong, crisp quality to speech. When they are not produced completely, speech can sound mushy or mumbly.

The *p* and *b* sounds are both made by pressing the lips together and then releasing them. The difference between them is that the *p* is voiceless (the vocal cords don't vibrate), and the *b* is voiced (vocal cords vibrate). To get a feel for this concept, put your fingers on your larynx (Adam's apple). Say *ah* and feel the vibration under your fingers—that sound is voiced. Now keep your fingers there and say *sh*. There is no vibration under your fingers because the sound is not voiced.

The *t* and *d* sounds are both made by bringing the tongue tip to the gum ridge (the bumpy area at the front of the roof of your mouth, just behind your upper teeth) and releasing. The *t* is voiceless, and the *d* is voiced. The *k* and *g* sounds are made by lifting the back of the tongue up to meet the soft palate (the back of the roof of the mouth), then releasing. The *k* is voiceless, and the *g* is voiced.

When a word ends with a plosive sound, many people stop before exploding the sound. For instance, in the word "stop," people often end the word with their lips closed. They start the *p* sound by building up the pressure behind their lips, but they don't release the air to make the sound audible.

Context dictates how forceful or subtle a plosive should be. If you are sitting next to someone in a quiet room, crisp speech might not be very important. If you are speaking to a group, however, or speaking over background noise or wanting to make a particular impression with your speech, strong diction is important.

On the Tip of Your Tongue

There are four sounds in English—*t, d, n,* and *l*—that require the tongue tip to come all the way up to the gum ridge. Many people have developed a habit of allowing the tongue tip to travel only part way up to the gum ridge, not making full, strong contact between these two articulators. Weak contact between the tongue and gum ridge on these four sounds leads to overall mushiness of speech.

The *t* sound is discussed in the plosive section above. The tongue tip presses against the gum ridge (careful not to touch the upper teeth!) and releases an explosion of air. The *d* sound, also discussed above, is the same as the *t* except that it's voiced.

The *n* sound is formed with the tongue in the same place, but the air is released in a different manner. Instead of being released explosively, it goes through the nose. You can't make the *n* sound—which is a nasal consonant—if your nose is stuffed up.

The *l* is also made with the tongue in the same place, but the air moves in yet another manner. It is a lateral sound, meaning that the sound comes out around the sides of your tongue. Of all of these sounds, the *l* is the one that most people consistently do not form fully. Remember that whenever an *l* sound occurs in a word, the tongue tip should press firmly against the gum ridge. It is important to form these sounds fully no matter where they appear in a word.

The More the Merrier

When two or more consonant sounds occur together, it is called a *consonant cluster*. People commonly leave out one or more of the consonants in a cluster. In order to speak clearly, you want to say all of the sounds in a word.

Consonant Sounds **8**

Practice the sounds discussed above along with the CD.

Plosives

Below are some words that end with plosive sounds. Practice completing the words so that the plosive sound really pops at the end. It might feel like you are exaggerating or speaking artificially at first. That's OK—any change feels odd in the beginning. Practicing a strong plosive will allow you to use varying degrees of intensity to suit your needs.

stop	bob
help	tube
ripe	ebb
keep	stub
right	ride
concept	load
late	bold
felt	loved
awake	big
look	rug
ask	egg
hike	bag
lake	

Tongue-Tip–Gum-Ridge Sounds

When the sounds *t*, *d*, *n*, and *l* appear at the beginning of a word, most people form them strongly, so we are going to focus on the middles and ends of words, where people tend to let these sounds slip.

T

beauty	eight
later	bright

D

meadow	divide
tidy	invaded

N

Phoenix	been
sunny	fireman

L

alligator	wall
biologist	feel

Consonant Clusters

Practice the following words with consonant clusters:

act	under
looked	end
raked	kindly
inject	fender
balked	binding
liked	winding

stopped	build
kept	kneeled
slipped	fooled
mopped	faint
rapt	mountain
stooped	painted
bold	pontoon
told	until
field	entertained
railed	

You've Got the Moves

A common habit that interferes with clear voice and speech is decreased mouth movement. A lot of people hold tension in the jaw and mouth, and the tension prevents the mouth from moving enough to make sounds accurately and clearly. Simply moving the mouth more can make speech, particularly vowels, sound clearer. There are two main mouth movements to work on expanding. One is the up-and-down movement of the jaw. The other is the movement of the lips and mouth muscles.

Mouth Calisthenics

These exercises can help train your mouth muscles to move with the precision, strength, and range of motion required for clear speech.

Open Wide   8

As you repeat the material below, keep both the up-and-down movement of the jaw and the movement of the lips and mouth muscles in mind. Exaggerate vertical jaw movement by opening your mouth very wide. Move your lips forward when possible, also exaggerating that motion. The goal of practice is not to sound natural but to train the muscles to work differently. Overdoing the movements in practice will help you retain the lesson when speaking in real life. When practicing, don't forget to apply the consonant work you have done as well!

my	look
may	loyal
moon	shine
put	rain
enjoyable	shoes
tiny	hook
tame	boy
tune	I
should	Shay
noisy	who
Einstein	could
able	oil
do	

I waited for a break.
Bob locked the door.
My friend Ray was late.
Who moved the glue?
Put the mail on the table.
Callie and Don had a baby boy.

Tongue Base Stretch

Stick your tongue out as far as you can, letting it move as far down your chin as possible. Hold for three deep breaths and release.

Strengthening the Tongue Tip

Open your jaw wide (look in a mirror to check yourself), and keep it there. Say *la la la la* repeatedly without moving your lower jaw. Feel free to use your hand to hold your jaw open. Don't let the jaw close as your tongue tip comes up to the gum ridge. Make sure the tongue moves all the way up and presses against the gum ridge to say the *l* sound, then moves all the way down to the floor of the mouth for the *ah* sound. Repeat as fast as you can while maintaining the accuracy of the sound and keeping your jaw wide. Do this for about 30 seconds.

Working the Back of the Tongue

Say *ka ka ka ka* repeatedly without moving your jaw, the same way you said *la* in the previous exercise. The back of the tongue touches the soft palate to make the *k* sound and comes all the way down to the bottom of the mouth to make the *ah* sound. Make sure the sound is a clear, crisp *ka* and is not mushy. Do this for about 30 seconds.

Energizing the Lips

Say *pa pa pa pa* over and over as fast as you can. Make sure the *p* sound is strong and muscular. Do this for about 30 seconds.

Engaging the Speech Muscles

Repeat the following sounds as fast as you can, 30 times each, with strong, exaggerated consonants:

ma	va
ta	da
ga	ba

Lip Range of Motion

Repeat *ooo eee ooo eee* with a full range of motion of the lips: Stretch the lips all the way forward for the *ooo* sound, and stretch them back for the *eee*. Do this about 30 times.

Additional mouth exercises can be found in chapter 9, "Preparing the Playing Field: Warm-Up and Cool-Down."

"Speak the Speech, I Pray You ..."

Once you have worked through the material in this chapter enough to have a feel for it, put it into practice. Read aloud from a book, newspaper, or computer screen, and focus on speaking clearly. If possible, record yourself and listen to the recording so you can learn how accurate your ear is while you are in the process of speaking. Practice using these techniques when you are projecting, presenting, or speaking over background noise. Use them with friends—you might be surprised by how little reaction you get. When you change your speech it feels drastic to you. But to others, even people who might live with you, the change is usually subtle or even unnoticeable.

If you are interested in more speech work, private voice and speech teachers can be of service; resources are listed in the appendix. There are also many excellent books and materials that focus on articulation in great depth.

Frequently Asked Questions about Articulation

Q: *People tell me I mumble. What does that mean?*

A: Mumbling generally refers to a lack of precision in your consonants. It also usually involves decreased movement in the jaw and other articulators. The overall energy of speech is dialed down a little bit. In addition to incomplete sound formation, mumbling often is also characterized by a decreased or monotone pitch range. Because of the general lack of vigor in mumbled speech, it is often too quiet to be heard easily.

   To counteract mumbling, you can use more breath to create a stronger sound, which in turn helps to energize your speech. As you practice reading aloud from anything you have handy, move your mouth more than you normally would and overarticulate. Make sure that you say every sound in a word. Once you have a feel for getting all the sounds in, visit chapter 6 to work on flowing your speech together so it is clear but not choppy.

   Mumbling can also project the image of lack of confidence. Chapter 11 has more information about giving the appearance of confidence when speaking.

Q: *Does speaking clearly mean speaking more slowly?*

A: Not necessarily. At first you might need to speak more slowly because you are learning a new skill, and your body needs a chance to catch up to your brain. We often learn a physical skill slowly (a dance step, a golf swing) before getting it up to speed. People often confuse speaking quickly with speaking imprecisely. Clients report being told by friends and colleagues that they speak too fast when, in reality, the problem is usually not the *speed* of their speech but rather the *clarity* of it. That being said, it takes longer to speak clearly than it does to mumble, which usually involves omitting some sounds. In other words, putting all the sounds in the words might slow you down if you are used to skipping some. If you are a very fast talker, you might want to slow down a bit anyway to give people a chance to keep up with you. This, however, is a different issue than speaking clearly. You can speak clearly and fast if you choose; how fast you go depends on your listener's ability to follow you.

8

Voice as a Metaphor

In this book, we focus primarily on the mechanics of voice production—anatomy, physiology, optimal use, and avoiding injury. But we would be remiss if we did not include some thoughts on voice as it fits into the bigger picture.

Figurative and Literal Voice

While rehabilitating voices, we have found that a person's "voice" in the world often parallels her voice quality. In other words, personality, emotion, and perceptions seem to influence voice quality. For example, a client came in for rehabilitation of vocal fold nodules. She was 32 years old and had been teaching general music and chorus for three elementary schools at once. She had become overwhelmed with her workload and felt unsupported by her administration. Even though she had expressed to her administration that she would accept no more than 80 students in her large choirs, the number continued to float up above 100. Additionally, she was helping students after school and felt that her extra efforts went unnoticed. A large aspect of her journey toward vocal health was to learn to draw boundaries and to self-advocate. She worked to recognize and accept her limitations and refuse to be a victim. She learned to say no without feeling guilty.

She empowered herself and took ownership of her own happiness and health. She was able to heal her nodules without surgery and continued to teach music.

Another of our clients was a singer with vocal fold polyps. During the course of therapy, it became clear to her that there was a connection between not expressing her feelings and opinions to her husband and her newly acquired throat tension. She observed that when she held back her thoughts, she felt tension in her throat. As she began to (bravely) speak up more in her primary relationship, her throat tensions diminished in general.

Yet another client discovered that speaking in a strong, resonant voice didn't match her self-image of a "cute, harmless" person. She also observed that supporting her voice with breath required a certainty or decisiveness that she purposefully omitted from her daily communication so as not to get flak for her opinions. These discoveries led her to release some old behavior patterns that no longer served her.

A surprising number of clients have suggested to us that the habitual tension they carry in the throat area might be related to something from the past, such as being told repeatedly and forcefully to be quiet as a child. Other issues that clients have identified as relating to their vocal problems include not wanting to be like a loud ("overbearing") parent, fear of saying the "wrong" thing, and a strong desire to avoid conflict and to keep the peace at all costs.

Challenges that you face when working with your voice are often representative of challenges you face in other areas. What are you learning from your voice?

We have observed that for many of our clients, their vocal tension seems to be connected to beliefs or behaviors born out of adapting to environmental pressures. Behaviors that are, or appear, necessary for survival at an early age can become destructive habits in adulthood. Some examples include suppressing one's truth, feeling trapped in a job or marriage, harboring unexpressed emotions, and believing that self-care is selfish.

One of our clients came to a session talking loudly and forcefully, with an overall air of urgency to his voice. He explained that his professional and personal lives had been hectic and rushed in the past week. The session ended up focusing on breathing, relaxation, and general stress management strategies. The client made reference on more than one occasion to enjoying the session despite its having "nothing to do with voice." He was told that the work had *everything* to do with voice. The following week, he started the session by describing an insight. He observed that when he became excited, enthusiastic, rushed, upset, or anxious, he held his breath. He further noted that this breath holding caused him to speak in the pressed, strained manner that led him to seek vocal coaching in the first place. Through awareness he learned the connection between emotion and voice.

Thoughts of anxiety, sadness, and anger can be felt physically in the throat with relative ease. Perhaps, then, *all* thoughts are actually affecting the throat. Our nervous system is designed to convey our state of arousal through vocal tone. This is evidenced by the fact that a baby's cry changes according to his intention. Furthermore, the human ear is designed to perceive nuances of the voice, as evidenced by a mother's ability to interpret a baby's cry. Tone of voice shows sarcasm, anger, surprise, love, joy, sadness, resolve, fatigue, anxiety, and a myriad of other complex emotional states. Voice training for actors capitalizes on our innate ability to express feeling through the voice by teaching students to explore the emotional colors this tool can offer.

The connection between voice and emotion is hardly surprising. We have expressions describing this phenomenon. Strong emotions give us a "lump in the throat." Irritating things get "stuck in our craw." And we get "all choked up" with unshed tears. Consider what personal experiences are influencing the quality of your voice.

> Common themes in voice development are "letting go" and patience with the process. How are you doing with those?

Voice as Energy

There is also a connection between voice and the energy in and around the human body. We can think of this type of energy as someone's "personal space" bubble. Most of us can tell if someone is standing very close to us even if we can't sense them with one of the five senses. One explanation for this is the energy field that surrounds the body. Just as sound travels through air as energy that we can't see, other subtle energies surround us as well. Many researchers over many decades have measured an electromagnetic field around the human body, often referring to it as an energy field or aura. Other scientists credit biophoton emission for the creation of the human energy field. In Ayurveda—the traditional medicine system of India—and many forms of complementary medicine and traditional healing, vortices in this energy field are referred to as *chakras*.

According to this system, there are seven major chakras along the torso and head, each one governing a different aspect of our being and corresponding to a major nerve ganglion branching from the spine. Not surprisingly, one of the chakras is located at the base of the throat. The throat chakra governs expression, creativity, and communication. The key issue for maintaining balance at the throat chakra is speaking your truth. Frequently "biting your tongue" instead of saying what's on your mind could, therefore, contribute to voice problems. While free expression appears to be the most powerful way to keep the throat chakra in balance, other tools the chakra system suggests for healing and balancing the throat chakra include wearing a blue stone at your throat (lapis, sodalite, azurite, turquoise); smelling frankincense, eucalyptus, and blue chamomile; and singing, toning, and chanting.

Exploring Your Voice from the Inside Out

Use the following journal questions to explore your relationship with your voice as well as your communication style. The intention of this exercise is for you to discover information about yourself that may be helpful in your journey to your authentic, free, and natural voice. Writing can open a window of opportunity to discover our motivations and beliefs. There truly are no right or wrong answers here, so release judgment and give your inner critic the day off when journaling about these topics. It might help the flow of your thoughts if you disregard spelling and grammatical rules while journaling. Relax and enjoy.

Journal Topics

1. Write your voice and speech autobiography. What factors influenced the way your voice developed? These factors might include geography, parents, peers, or role models.

2. Finding and connecting to your authentic voice is inextricably linked to being your authentic self. To what extent are you your authentic self in the world?

3. How do you handle conflict? Do you confront, explode, hide, or something else? How does your throat feel during times of conflict?

4. Self-talk governs much of our behavior, often subconsciously. Can you identify a common theme in the "tape" that runs in your head that may affect your self-expression?

5. Have you had positive or negative experiences in your life that have manifested in your voice quality and your willingness to explore it?

6. Growing up, were you praised for expressing yourself? Or were you told to shut up?

7. How much of what you do comes from fear versus expectation of opportunity and reward?

8. What creative outlets do you have? Consider ways to express, create, and play that would fit into your life.

9. Can you think of at least one aspect of voice as a metaphor that has resonance for you? Is there one area of your Voice, in the largest sense, that could use some attention?

9

Preparing the Playing Field: Warm-Up and Cool-Down

The students in a college course called Voice for the Actor offer a clear example of the value of a vocal warm-up. They were asked to perform their prepared speeches at the beginning of class with no warm-up. Then they were led through a 20-minute vocal warm-up (the one outlined in this chapter) focusing on releasing physical tension, connecting the voice to deep breath, warming up the vocal fold muscles, and enhancing resonance. They performed their speeches again and were asked to describe the differences, if any, that they felt between the two performances. They uniformly noted improvement in vocal quality, ease of speaking, or both. Many were surprised by the extent of the difference, citing changes such as increased projection, range, variety, power, breath support, ease and comfort in the throat, and overall energy.

Just as you wouldn't run a race without warming up your muscles, it is important to warm up the voice before a *vocal* workout. If you plan to use your voice heavily for the better part of the day, we recommend that you warm up in the morning. You may find that it is also useful to repeat your warm-up exercises just before a vocally athletic activity. Such activity could include prolonged talking, loud talking, yelling, cheering, or talking over background noise. Generally, for optimal effect, a vocal warm-up should be done no more than an hour before the vocally demanding event. Even a "quick and dirty" warm-up immediately before speaking is better than nothing.

The frequency of warm-ups depends on what you actually need to do with your voice. For daily life, many people can get through the day perfectly well without warming up. However, most people who are doing the work in this book have some kind of vocally athletic or vocally demanding work. In that case, a daily warm-up is advisable.

It is also important to *cool down* your voice after any vocally strenuous activity. This chapter will guide you through both activities.

The Warm-Up

The goal of your vocal warm-up is to optimize your alignment and breathing patterns for speech as well as to tune your voice to its most resonant, comfortable timbre. By doing a vocal warm-up in the morning, you are showing your body how you would like your voice to sound and feel during speech for the entire day. Small "check-in" sessions with your voice throughout the day are also helpful in overcoming pesky habits that may creep into your muscles, causing problems such as jaw tension, chin jut posture, throat tension, or shallow breathing.

The CD outlines a complete vocal warm-up. We suggest that you read through the following explanation of the exercises to familiarize yourself with the concepts before listening to it. Then put the book down and allow the CD to guide you through the warm-up. We assume you have worked through the exercises in the previous chapters already.

Warm-Up Exercises, Part I: Musculature 9

Neck Stretches

1. Roll your head forward, then gently swing your head from side to side (figure 9-1).

Figure 9-1: Neck stretches

2. To stretch the front of your neck, stick your lower jaw out (so that your bottom teeth are in front of your top teeth). Now, tip your head back and reach toward the ceiling with your chin (figure 9-2). Hold for three breaths. Now reach your chin toward the left side of the ceiling. Hold for one breath. Now aim your chin toward the right side of the ceiling. Hold for one breath. Return to center.

Figure 9-2: Stretching the front of the neck

3. To stretch the sides of your neck, wrap your left arm up and over the top of your head so that your left palm is touching your right ear. Let the weight of your arm tilt your head to the left as far as is comfortable and feel the stretch on the right side of your neck (figure 9-3). Reach down to the ground with your right fingertips so that your right shoulder lowers. Hold for three breaths. Leave your head where it is, let your hands relax and

let your head gently float back to center. Repeat on the other side, i.e., right palm over left ear.

4. To stretch the back of neck, clasp your fingers together in front of you, drop your chin down to your chest, and bring your hands around to the crown of your head. Let the weight of your hands and arms deepen the stretch (figure 9-4). Make sure your knees are unlocked. You might feel a stretch down your back as well. Hold for three breaths.

Figure 9-3: Side neck stretch

Jaw Massage

1. Put your fingers on the part of your face directly in front your ears. Open and close your mouth and feel for movement. This hinge is the jaw joint, or temporomandibular joint (TMJ). With your jaw relaxed, gently massage that joint (figure 9-5). Do this for about 10 seconds.

2. Next, move to the masseter muscle, the jaw-closing muscle, which is, fiber for fiber, the strongest muscle in the human body. Put your hand over your jawbone underneath your ear, and clench and unclench your teeth as though you were chewing. Feel for a bulge. Relax your jaw and then massage that muscle bulge for about 10 seconds.

Figure 9-4: Stretching the back of the neck

Figure 9-5: Massaging the temporomandibular joint

3. There is another part of this muscle that is a little harder to reach as it is up under the cheekbone. Press your fingers into the part of your cheek right above the corners of your lips so you are pressing on your teeth. Then, slide your fingers up and back into the corner underneath your cheekbone (figure 9-6). Clench your teeth and feel for a little bulge. Unclench your teeth and massage for 10 seconds up in that corner. This muscle is often tender.

Figure 9-6: Massaging the masseter muscle under the cheekbones

4. With the heels of your hands, apply comfortable, steady pressure starting at the temporomandibular joint and sliding down the jawbone to the point of the chin. Sweep all the tension in your jaw out the point of your chin. Let your jaw be so relaxed that the pressure of your hands causes it to passively open, as though you are ironing the tension out of your jaw. Repeat three times.

5. Take the palms of your hands and place them on the sides of your face. Move your hands forward so that your thumbs gently slide under your chin on both sides. Now move your thumbs up and down into the soft area underneath your chin like a cat kneading a blanket (figure 9-7). Continue for 10 seconds.

Figure 9-7: Kneading the muscles under the jaw

Tongue Exercises

1. Try to touch your nose with your tongue. Keep your jaw relaxed and avoid letting it move forward to "help." Hold for three deep breaths (figure 9-8).

Figure 9-8: Stretching the tongue up

2. Stick your tongue out, down your chin as far as it will go, and hold for about 10 seconds. Keep your jaw relaxed (figure 9-9). Notice whether your jaw feels tight as you do this, and release it if it does. When you bring your tongue back into your mouth, notice that it naturally returns to the resting position of lying low and flat. This stretch is a good way to find that low, flat tongue position.

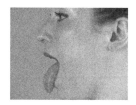

Figure 9-9: Stretching the tongue down

3. Stick your tongue out straight, parallel to the ground, without it touching your lower teeth or lips, and hold for 10 seconds (figure 9-10). You may need to use a mirror to check—it's easy to accidentally rest the tongue on the bottom teeth. Keep your face relaxed. If you can't hold your tongue out, start by holding it straight but back farther in your mouth. As your

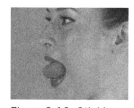

Figure 9-10: Sticking the tongue straight out

tongue gets stronger, you'll gradually be able to inch it forward without needing the lower teeth for support.

Are you breathing?

4. Tongue curls. Open your mouth and keep it open. You may need to hold your jaw with your hand to keep it from moving. Anchor your tongue tip behind your bottom teeth and keep it there for the whole exercise. Now, roll the back of your tongue out the front of your mouth (figure 9-11). Then without your jaw closing, lay your tongue completely flat, down, and back (figure 9-12). Use a mirror to check this position. You should be able to see your uvula and the back of your throat when your tongue is flat. Work with this until you get it. If you can't get your tongue flat, try yawning to see the back of your throat. There is a learning curve with this exercise. Don't give up. Repeat five times.

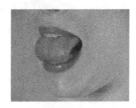

Figure 9-11: Curling the tongue forward out the mouth

Figure 9-12: Laying the tongue flat in the mouth

Alignment

Check your head position and allow your neck to be long and straight in the back. Your ears are centered over your shoulders, giving the sensation that your head is resting on top of your spine and that the weight of your head is supported from above (figure 9-13).

Figure 9-13: Aligned head, side and front view

Warm-Up Exercises, Part II: Breathing 9

Low Expansion Inhale

1. Hug yourself and bend over comfortably; breathe into your back for five breaths.

2. Extend your right arm up and over your head and lean over to the left, stretching the muscles on the right side of your torso. Breathe into those stretched muscles three times. Feel your rib cage expand with your breath. Repeat on the other side.

3. Pant like a puppy from the abdomen for 10 seconds. Make sure the sound doesn't "come from" the throat.

Fff Exercise

1. Let all of your breath out while sustaining a *fff* sound. Feel your stomach move in as you do this. (The stomach moves in automatically at first, then you help it.)

2. Wait as long as you can, but don't hold your breath by tightening your throat. Just wait.

3. When you can't wait any longer, let your stomach muscles quickly pop out, and feel the air "rush into" your abdominal area. Let this breath in through the mouth.

4. Repeat five times.

Are your shoulders relaxed?

Adding Speech to Breath

Count from 1 to 50, alternating the length of breath groups. For example, you might count like this: 1–3 (breath), 4–9 (breath), 10–19 (breath), 20–21 (breath), etc. Make some groups of numbers short, some medium, and some long (like conversational speech). Be sure to breathe in through your mouth and feel your belly move out.

Warm-Up Exercises, Part III:
Warming Up the Vocal Folds 9

Hum and Chew

1. Chew as though you have a large piece of bubble gum in your mouth. Explore your jaw's full range of mobility while maintaining closure between your lips.

2. Hum as you chew slowly, and feel the vibrations move around your mouth.

3. Pay special attention to the vibration in the bone above your upper lip.

4. Vary your pitch as you hum. Do this exercise for about 30 seconds.

Puppy Dog Whimper

1. Say the word "sing" and linger on the *ng* sound at the end of the word. This sound is made with the back of the tongue touching the soft palate.

2. On the *ng* sound, make a sound like a puppy whining as though he were asking to be let in from outside.

3. Explore with the puppy dog whimper throughout your pitch range, allowing your own comfort level to dictate how high and low you go.

Sirens

1. On an *ng* sound, make a sound at the lowest pitch that you are capable of producing without discomfort.

2. Gently glide your pitch upward to the very highest pitch you can comfortably make and then back down to the lowest pitch. The effect is similar to a siren.

3. Strive for consistency in volume as you go throughout your comfortable range. You might notice voice breaks as the muscles in the larynx "shift gears." With practice, the transition can become smooth.

4. Repeat the exercise five times, or until it is easy and smooth.

Lip Trills

1. Take in a deep breath and then make an unvoiced "raspberry" sound with your lips, like a horse. Do this three times.

2. Add voice to your raspberry so it sounds like a motorboat. This is a "voiced lip trill," and it is an excellent vocal warm-up.

3. Use the voiced lip trill to siren through your range as in the last exercise.

4. Next, freely explore different pitches without structure, moving randomly around your pitch range. You can even lip trill a favorite melody. (You will probably feel a tickle in your nose or lips.)

Decrease Tongue Tension

1. Place your thumb underneath your chin into the soft area below your jaw. It is best to keep the muscles in this area loose when you use your voice. When they contract, you will feel a hardening of the area and your thumb will be pushed down.

2. Take in a breath and hold out the sound *ooo* as long as is comfortable.

3. Once you are able to do this without tightening the muscles behind the bony part of your chin, try it using different pitches and vowel sounds.

1-to-20 Counting

Count from 1 to 20, alternating your lowest-pitched speaking voice with your highest-pitched speaking voice, including falsetto for men. Odd numbers are at the low end of your comfortable range and even numbers are at the top.

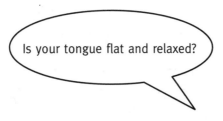
Is your tongue flat and relaxed?

Humming into Resonators

1. Place your hands on your chest and hum. Feel the amount of vibration in your chest that you can create there.

2. Now gently place one finger between your nose and upper lip (the mustache zone). Hum and feel the vibration there. See how much vibration you can generate.

3. Gently place your hands so that your palms are on your cheekbones and your fingers are resting on your forehead. Hum and feel how much vibration you can produce in these bones.

4. Place your hands on top of your head. Hum and create vibration there.

Warm-Up Exercises, Part IV:
Forward Focus and Articulation   9

Forward Focus Progression

1. Starting in the rest position (head aligned, jaw relaxed, and tongue flat), say *mm-hmm*, as though agreeing with something. Feel the vibration in your maxilla. Remember that we called this sound your "anchor" in the resonance chapter.

2. Say *hmm*, as though pondering something.

3. Exaggerating the *m* and *n* sounds so you can feel the maxillary vibration strongly, say the following words/phrases (or make up your own words that start with *m* or *n*).

Moon	No one knew me
Man	No one knew me in Maine
Many	No way
No	My way
No one	Never mind
No one knew	Million

4. Say the word "hum" and linger on the *m* until you feel the vibration in the maxilla. Let the word come out of you in an arc as opposed to a straight line.

5. Repeat the following sequence, maintaining the feeling of vibration in the maxilla while you sustain the *m* in "hum."

> HummmOne
> HummmOneTwo
> HummmOneTwoThree
> HummmOneTwoThreeFour
> HummmOneTwoThreeFourFive

6. Still focusing on the vibration of the *m* sound and the arc, say:

> HummmAnd then a sentence you make up
> (i.e., "HummmIt's a beautiful day")

7. Make up several sentences to say in this way. Feel the sentence "coming from" the front of your face.

Is your jaw relaxed?

8. Repeat steps 6 and 7 above, and this time after you finish each sentence, take a breath and then say the same sentence again *without* the "hum" before it (i.e., "HummmIt's cold in here" — breathe in — "It's cold in here"). Intend that the second repetition of the sentence stays in the same place as the first (resonating in the bone above upper lip).

9. Talk to yourself in short sentences with the intention of keep-
    ing your voice forward. Sense vibration in the maxilla, or the
    feeling of the sound "coming from" the front of your mouth as
    opposed to your throat.

Tongue Twisters

Say the following sentences while exaggerating your articulation and mouth movement. All consonants should be produced
very crisply. Let your mouth move more than it does in regular
speech.

> Toy boat, toy boat, toy boat, toy boat.
> Peter Piper picked a peck of pickled peppers. If
>   Peter Piper picked a peck of pickled peppers,
>   where's the peck of pickled peppers Peter
>   Piper picked?
> Red leather yellow leather.
> The big black bug bit the big black bear and the
>   big black bug drew blood.
> She sells seashells by the seashore.

The Cool-Down

After strenuous activity, it is important to cool down your voice
in part because lactic acid is produced in muscles during exertion, and cooling down the muscles helps to disperse the lactic
acid so that it doesn't build up and diminish the muscles' ability to function. It is also helpful to return your voice to a state
of calm and unstrained use. We often observe that once someone begins speaking loudly, the tendency is to continue speaking
loudly even when it is not necessary. By cooling down your voice,
you can overcome this natural tendency to continue overexerting

your voice. As one of our teachers, Bonnie Raphael, said, "The cool-down is like putting your toys back in the box when you are finished playing with them."

Cool-Down Exercises

1. With your eyes closed, do a quick body check, and coach your body to low and steady abdominal breathing, released shoulders, and an open vocal tract. Allow your jaw and tongue to return to the rest position.

2. Do a couple of forward and side head rolls to stretch your neck. Stick your tongue out and stretch the back of your tongue. Take a few deep breaths and allow your breathing to return to the low, centered part of your body.

3. Do some very gentle humming, still feeling the vibration in the maxilla.

4. To "reset" your voice to a comfortable level, take an easy abdominal breath. Then while focusing your sound forward, say a few commonly used phrases. For example, "Hello, this is [say your name]," or "How are you?" Use a loudness level appropriate for a quiet location.

5. Sip some water. If you don't have any nearby, chew your tongue to generate saliva.

Frequently Asked Questions about Warm-Up and Cool-Down

Q: I seem to be doing OK without warming up; why do I suddenly need to start?

A: Depending on the nature of your vocal use, this could be comparable to saying, I walk around just fine every day, so why do

I need to stretch before running a marathon? The answer lies in what your vocal needs are. Just because you have been able to get through your day without warming up thus far, that doesn't mean that you are necessarily using the system in the most effective or efficient way. The program outlined in this book is one of optimizing vocal efficiency. A warm-up is part of that process.

Q: *Should I use the CD to warm up my voice or can I do it on my own?*

A: It is advisable to use the CD to learn your warm-up well before attempting it from memory. By doing the warm-up using only the written instructions provided in this book, it is possible you will miss some nuances that can only be communicated by listening to somebody completing the task. Once you feel that you have mastered the techniques using the CD, you certainly can do your warm-up without it. In fact, you are encouraged to personalize it so that it works for you.

Q: *Should I warm up even if I am sick?*

A: This depends upon how sick you are and also what you are going to do that day. If your plans were to rest and recover, then a vocal warm-up would not be of service to you. If, however, you plan to use your voice while sick, the vocal warm-up is actually an excellent tool for you to use to see if your larynx has been affected by your illness. If during your vocal warm-up you notice that voicing is particularly difficult, strenuous, or painful, it is advised that you follow voice precautions throughout the day. (See chapter 10 for more information about "checking in" with the status of your vocal cords.) In other words, rest and keep your conversations short so that you don't cause any damage. Vocal warm-ups can be helpful in reminding you to use plenty of air during this time and to relax your body even though you are feeling ill. They also help achieve the desired effect of "talking over" the swelling in your vocal folds. Some of the exercises in the warm-up may actually help to diminish swelling due to the action of the vocal folds.

Many people feel as though they should speak differently when they are sick and that the forward placement that we have been working toward is inadvisable during illness. This is not true. It is all the more important to speak in this forward, supported way when you have any swelling on your vocal folds. Even though the resonant voice is more powerful, it is healthier than talking in the low, throaty, breathy voice that many people use during illness in a misguided attempt to "rest" the voice. Therefore, although it is counterintuitive, forward placement is usually the healthiest way to use your voice whether you are sick or not. The bottom line is if you are going to use your voice anyway, this is a good way to do it and the warm-up will help you. If, however, you feel uncertain of your ability to achieve forward placement without pushing, you might want to seek additional coaching. It's also true that laryngitis can make it impossible for you to use your voice healthily no matter how good your technique.

Q: *If I just do the warm-up every day, will I reach optimum vocal efficiency?*

A: The warm-up is a good start. The way to achieve optimum voicing is to master the exercises in each chapter in this book and use those techniques in your daily speech (which requires conscious attention in the beginning). Some individuals will need additional daily work on breath awareness in order to habituate abdominal breathing during speech. Others may need additional work on forward focus. You can design your daily vocal practice to meet your particular needs for achieving optimal vocal efficiency.

10

Safeguarding the Valuables: Preventing Vocal Injury

A successful young recording artist was on tour when she lost the top half of her singing range. Over the previous year, she had engaged in behaviors that were harmful to her voice, such as smoking, drinking a lot of alcohol and caffeine and not enough water, singing without a monitor, and singing out of her range. Because of this, she began to gradually lose the top octave of her singing voice. Instead of seeking treatment right away, she compensated by straining and yelling to try to hit them. This only made her condition worse. When she finally sought help, her therapy focused on releasing the strain she had developed in her throat muscles over years of misuse. She also lowered the keys of her songs so she would not have to strain to hit the notes. While she regained some of her range, she was unable to return to performing and recording.

But that's not the way the story had to turn out. Consider the situation of a young second-grade teacher who developed vocal nodules. She was hoarse by Thursday every week, and had so much discomfort with voice use that she didn't want to talk after school. She was sure she would not be able to maintain her voice and her career. Therapy for her focused on resonance, linking and easy onset, maintaining adequate hydration, and reducing loudness. She also used an amplifier in the classroom so she would not have to speak as loudly. Her colleagues complimented her on how much better she sounded after therapy, and she was no longer hoarse or tired. By changing her behaviors relatively early on, she was able to save her voice.

How Vocal Folds Get Damaged

A vocal injury can be defined as a wound to the vocal folds. Vocal injuries usually cause symptoms such as hoarseness, breathiness, loss of singing range, breaks in the voice, lack of stamina required for extended voicing, and a feeling of vocal strain/fatigue. Some vocal injuries are caused by the way the voice is used, and others are caused by genetic factors, trauma, or a breakdown in the nervous system. Because vocal behavior is controllable, we are going to focus on those disorders that are caused by the way a voice is used.

There are four common use-related injuries to the vocal folds. *Nodules* are similar to hard calluses. *Polyps* are similar to water blisters. *Edema* (swelling) is fluid retention in the vocal folds. Many nodules and polyps start as edema. *Hemorrhage* (bruise) is a bleed in the vocal folds due to a burst blood vessel.

Developing a little bit of swelling on the vocal folds from voice use is like getting a blister from wearing an ill-fitting shoe. If you get a little irritation from wearing the shoe and then you stop wearing it, the injury heals. However, if you keep wearing that shoe over and over again and you never let that little irritation heal, it may become a blister or a callus. The same is true for the vocal folds. We all experience a little bit of vocal fold swelling from time to time, be it from an exuberant day at the stadium or from illness. After we rest, our voices usually return to normal as the swelling subsides. If, however, we continue to yell, or if we insist on using our voices even when our vocal folds are swollen from illness, the swelling can become more permanent.

If the vocal folds are not allowed to rest and the swelling is not allowed to heal, then the cells on the vocal folds begin to think that a tougher protective layer is needed to withstand all the impact force from the vibration. That is when the actual material in the vocal folds begins to change and toughen, becoming stiffer and harder. This leads to a permanent loss of vocal clarity.

Swelling and blistering of an area of skin is usually the result of too much impact stress in that area. This is true of the vocal folds as well. The harder the vocal folds hit each other, the more heat is generated—particularly at the midpoint of the vibrating vocal folds. The midpoint is where the vocal folds hit each other the hardest during vibration, and is therefore the place of greatest impact force. As a result, that area tends to be the place where polyps and nodules occur, in response to excessive impact force and heat.

There are three main factors that play into how much impact stress is generated in the vocal folds when you use your voice.

1. *How you use your voice.* Three vocal use patterns that appear to increase the impact force between your vocal folds are: elevated vocal volume (caused by increased air pressure below the vocal folds), elevated vocal pitch (created by vocal fold elongation), and vocal fold pressing (caused by the arytenoids closing the vocal folds too hard). Therefore, if you commonly produce a loud, high, strained voice, you are likely generating large impact stress. This is why screaming is often associated with nodules, and probably why it is more common for a soprano to develop nodules than for a bass. Some people also have a weakness in the nerve that feeds the vocal folds (*vocal fold paresis*). Paresis can be caused by genetics, virus, or trauma/injury, and can lead to compensatory

speaking behaviors that can cause damage to the vocal fold tissue.

2. *Dehydration.* When the gelatinous tissue in your vocal folds becomes dry and irritated, vibration of this area is more likely to promote friction. Increased friction leads to increased heat, which may cause vocal injury.

3. *Genetics.* Each one of us has a different level of tolerance before the vocal folds become swollen. This may be genetically predetermined and appears to be related to the sturdiness of the elastin and collagen fibers in an area of the vocal folds called the *basement membrane zone.* The less sturdy they are, the more likely they are to break down in the face of extensive vocal use and dehydration. When they break down, there is usually swelling and perhaps stiffness, both of which negatively impact vocal quality.

The good news is that you can learn to use your voice in such a way that the vocal folds don't bang together strongly, but rather close completely and gently. That way they don't generate the excessive impact stresses, friction, and heat that can lead to swelling and other injuries. The following sections explain the hows and whys.

The Wetter the Better

Hydration, for our purposes, refers to keeping the vocal fold tissue adequately moist. Maintaining sufficient moisture in the vocal folds is one of the primary ways in which you can keep your vocal fold tissue healthy. Vocal folds that are well hydrated are less likely to produce a lot of friction upon vibrating, and therefore generate less edema-provoking heat. One quick and easy way that you can prepare your vocal folds for the vibration of extensive voice use is to make sure that they are as hydrated as possible.

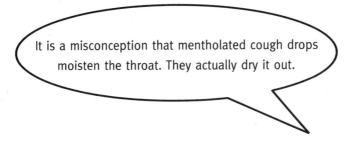

It is a misconception that mentholated cough drops moisten the throat. They actually dry it out.

When the vocal folds vibrate, they move in a wavelike fashion—they ripple. We therefore want them to be as supple as possible. Just like anything else, when they are dry, they lose their suppleness and don't ripple as well. Consider paint or nail polish as it starts to dry out—it becomes less runny, becoming thicker and stickier. It doesn't have the same fluidity it had when it was properly hydrated. The same is true for the tissue of the vocal folds. Like a sponge, the vocal folds are more pliable when wet and stiffer when dry.

In order to keep properly hydrated, there are three approaches to consider. The first and most important is drinking water. In many disparate fields of Eastern and Western medicine, one thing that most experts seem to agree on is that we need to drink plenty of water. So the old standby of eight eight-ounce glasses of water a day (a half-gallon, two liters) is probably adequate for most people. If you do things that dry you out over and above normal daily living, to be discussed below, then you may require even more water. There are no two ways about it: we need to drink water, and we need to drink more of it than most of us do. One guideline for determining the amount of water your body needs is the "pee pale" yardstick. If your urine is almost colorless, your body is allowing water to pass through your system, and you are probably adequately hydrated.

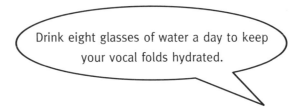

Drink eight glasses of water a day to keep your vocal folds hydrated.

The second way to maintain adequate hydration of the vocal folds is to inhale steam. When you drink water you are not hydrating the vocal folds directly. The water doesn't really touch the vocal folds, which sit on top of the airway. Rather, it goes *behind* the airway, down the esophagus into your stomach, and enters the vocal folds systemically. The only way that you can actually get any moisture directly on the vocal folds is to breathe it in. Remember, everything that you breathe in touches the vocal folds on the way down to the lungs. So breathing in steam essentially bathes the outer layer of the vocal folds in moisture, which is a nice thing to do for them.

Direct steam inhalation can be accomplished in a few ways. One is to place your face over a pot of recently boiled water (taken off the burner!), create a tent with a towel to trap the steam, and breathe in and out through your nose and mouth. More convenient are portable inhalers, available in many drug stores, that generate gentle steam and have a plastic device to direct the steam to the face and to regulate the amount and temperature of the steam. A steam room is another option, as long as you drink enough water to replace fluids lost by sweating. Even being in a steamy shower generates some steam for inhalation, though not as much as the other alternatives. Conversely, saunas are usually drying and might have a negative impact on vocal fold moisture. Use of a hot water vaporizer/humidifier in your bedroom at night is also a good way to deliver moistened air to your vocal folds.

The third way to maintain proper hydration is to avoid drying agents. Consuming diuretics, or things that encourage your body to pass water out of your system, is a common way of drying out the vocal folds. The most common diuretics are alcohol, caffeine, and some medications. You may notice that after drinking a couple of cups of coffee in the morning, you have an urge to urinate. The same thing happens after drinking alcohol. You are passing water out of your body, thereby causing drying of the internal tissue. In fact, dehydration plays a large role in hangovers. So minimizing, or at least compensating for, alcohol and caffeine consumption is an important way to maintain systemic (and therefore vocal fold) hydration. If you do consume alcohol and caffeine in moderation, you can then increase the amount of water that you drink to help to maintain the hydration of your body (i.e., for each glass of wine, have an extra glass of water).

Many medications can dry out your vocal folds. Check www.ncvs.org for a listing of medications and their effects on voice.

Vocal Cord Enemies

There are many frequently encountered substances that can irritate the tissue of the vocal folds, thereby making them more vulnerable to injury.

Smoke and Other Drying Agents

As noted previously, everything we breathe goes past the vocal cords and touches them on the way to the lungs. Irritating substances such as smoke from cigarettes and cigars, stage smoke, and artificial fog can dry out the vocal cords. Even just breathing in super-dry air, such as on an airplane or in a room with forced air, can dry out the vocal folds. The effect is similar to that of an evaporative cooler. As the dry air or smoke passes over the moist vocal folds, it "borrows" some of the moisture from the vocal folds on its way down to the lungs.

> Cigarettes pose *huge* risk to the health of your vocal folds, not to mention your lungs. Smoke and fumes cause irritation, swelling, and sometimes lesions on the vocal folds, leading to permanent hoarseness and voice loss.

Reflux

Acid reflux, or stomach acid coming back up from the stomach to the throat, is a surprisingly common vocal fold irritant. The esophagus is designed to squeeze food down into the stomach. There is a sphincter between the esophagus and the stomach that tightens and keeps all of the stomach contents where they belong so they can be digested. In some cases, the process of moving food down to the stomach and keeping it there can malfunction, and stomach acid and other stomach contents can come right back up the esophagus. This can cause sensations that we refer to as "heartburn," "acid indigestion," or "sour stomach." These are issues that people commonly recognize as symptoms of acid reflux. What few people understand is that it is also possible to have reflux that comes up into your throat and causes irritation to your throat *without* symptoms of heartburn or sour stomach.

Reflux that occurs primarily at the level of the throat has a slightly different name than garden-variety reflux. Regular reflux is referred to as *gastroesophageal reflux disease*, or GERD. Reflux occurring at the level of your larynx, however, is called *laryngopharyngeal reflux*, or LPR. Symptoms of LPR include:

- Hoarseness
- Excessive mucus in the morning
- Dry cough
- Sharp, burning pain at the level of the larynx
- A sensation of a lump in your throat
- Belching
- Really bad breath or a bitter taste at the back of your throat when you wake up
- Voice taking more than 15 minutes or so to warm up in the morning

It is also possible to have "silent reflux," which is reflux without any obvious symptoms. At times, hoarseness or excessive phlegm are the only perceivable symptoms of LPR.

The reason people with LPR might not perceive any kind of heartburn is because the esophagus is designed to withstand a little bit of stomach acid without it being problematic. The larynx, however, is not designed to withstand any amount of acid. So the smallest amount of acid on the larynx is very irritating. It is like putting a drop of Tabasco on the skin of your hand versus putting a drop of it on your eyeball. One is clearly designed to be much more sensitive than the other.

For many people the result of LPR is redness, irritation, and swelling of the vocal folds. In addition, acid in the larynx can disrupt our ability to unconsciously feel things like where vocal folds are in space and how we need to move them. The result of that disruption is that we are more likely to squeeze too much and put too much pressure on the larynx because our innate sense of how the structures are moving and responding is altered by the irritant.

To minimize the possibility of having LPR, consider the fact that the following activities may contribute to reflux:

- Eating large amounts at once
- Eating spicy foods, fried foods, and acidic foods (like citrus or tomato-based foods)
- Wearing clothing with tight waist bands
- Bending at the waist
- Eating within three to four hours of lying down (some people elevate the head of their bed with bricks so that gravity assists in keeping acid away from the larynx)
- Sleeping on your belly
- Exercising right after eating
- Drinking caffeine and alcohol

Maintain good overall nutrition.

Postnasal Drip

Postnasal drip occurs when thick secretions drip down from the nose to the back of the throat. These secretions often arrive at or near the vocal folds, causing irritation. This irritation leads to discomfort and the need to cough. Frequent coughing can result in vocal injury. Postnasal drip can be managed with the aid of a physician. Regular use of a nasal saline spray (not medicated nose sprays) can thin out your postnasal secretions.

The average nose generates a quart of mucous a day. It is when this mucous becomes thickened or more copious that we perceive postnasal drip.

Environmental Irritants

Common environmental irritants can cause redness and swelling of some people's vocal folds, depending on their sensitivities. These irritants include chemical fumes, dust, mold, and other allergens. If you are exposed to any of these on a regular basis (including cleaning supplies, dust, mold, nail polish remover, paint, and paint thinner), be aware that they might be having a negative effect on your voice. Always use a face mask when confronted with these irritants. If you regularly feel a burning sensation in your throat or you develop hoarseness when exposed to these substances, you should seek the help of a physician.

Beauty Rest

Rest your voice when it feels tired. Pace yourself. Imagine that you have a vocal budget that you can use every day without becoming hoarse. If you have heavy vocal use planned for the afternoon, rest your voice in the morning in anticipation of that. Or if you have to talk for eight hours during the day, take intermittent breaks to rest your voice. Muscles need to rest in order to remain strong, and the outer layer of vocal fold tissue needs a break from vibration in order to avoid swelling.

Know your vocal limits. Learn what your voice can do, and always stop if you feel fatigued.

Don't Slam the Cords!

Common behaviors that can cause the vocal cords to slam together are throat clearing, strained yelling, strained screaming, Valsalva (hyperclosure of the larynx when bearing down), and extensive talking or singing without breaks. Even some ways of talking can cause enough impact force to create an injury in some people.

With impact force, the capillaries in the vocal folds can burst, causing a hemorrhage. Aspirin and ibuprofen both have properties that make the capillaries more prone to bursting. Women are at greater risk of a vocal fold hemorrhage during menstruation.

Clearing your throat is grinding the vocal folds together to clear mucous while they are trying to vibrate. That is not good for them. Throat clearing becomes habituated in some people and can occur without conscious awareness. To determine if you are a habitual throat clearer, tally every time you clear your throat in a day. If you are clearing more than a few times in the absence of illness, you may be doing so habitually.

In general, if you must clear, the softer the better. You can gently tap your vocal folds together to remove the mucus without trying to make sound at the same time (similar to a gentle cough). It is the act of bumping them together and trying to have them vibrate simultaneously that causes the majority of the problem. Other ways to clear mucus are to sniff sharply and then swallow so that the mucus is pulled down into the esophagus, or to hold the vocal folds apart and blow air through the throat, as demonstrated on track 11 on the CD.

During weight lifting or other physically strenuous activity, be especially careful of grunting. Squeezing the vocal folds together when we lift something heavy or bear down can irritate them. Be conscious of exhaling just before and during exertion to keep the strain out of your throat. This has the added benefit of directing the energy to the muscles you mean to strengthen instead of the throat muscles.

> Moving cars are noisy. Watch for vocal fatigue and strain when talking in a car.

Amp It Up

Amplification is a good way to reduce the vocal fold impact stress. Many professional voice users (such as coaches, teachers, and fitness instructors) need to speak for an extended time over background noise. They often grow accustomed to this noise and don't notice that they are talking loudly. Using a microphone and amplification system will help take some of the wear and tear off the vocal folds by producing the loudness externally.

Compact, battery-operated voice amplification systems are available for around $200. These systems, such as the ChatterVox or SoniVox (see the appendix for more information) require the user to wear a small pack around the waist and a headset microphone. The loudspeaker is located within the waist pack, and the only cord is the one running from the microphone to the pack. These systems are light, hands free, and allow the user to be completely mobile.

Use It So You Don't Lose It

The program outlined in this book is designed to promote efficient speech. In a nutshell, this is accomplished by:

- Taking in adequate breath before speaking (using low abdominal breathing rather than high, shallow, or tight breath), then replenishing that breath before your larynx becomes "air starved" at the ends of phrases.
- Releasing tension in your larynx and vocal tract through alignment and conscious relaxation of the tongue, jaw, throat, neck, and shoulders.
- Using forward resonance while talking. This promotes full closure of the vocal folds and minimizes impact force as they close. It also maximizes the acoustic benefits of the vocal tract.

Pressed or strained voice, speaking with inadequate breath support, throat-focused resonance, and speaking at an unnatural pitch level can cause the vocal folds to hit each other in a way than is not ideal. The intention of this book is to encourage the production of voice such that the vocal folds close completely and gently along their full length with minimal impact force and, therefore, minimal damage.

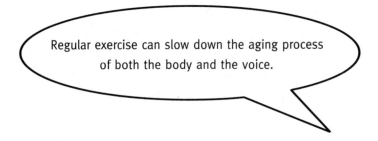

Regular exercise can slow down the aging process of both the body and the voice.

Danger Signs

As mentioned previously, the amount of vibration a pair of vocal folds is able to withstand before becoming swollen varies from one person to the next. Therefore, you may find that you are able to speak for eight hours without becoming hoarse or fatigued. However, your friend may only be able to speak for six hours. This variable threshold each of us has for speaking is due to genetics, voice use, and tissue integrity. Beyond this point, our speaking becomes injurious. It is important to know the warning signs of vocal injury so you understand when your voice needs a rest.

Some common warning signs of a vocal injury are:

- *Lowering of speaking or preferred singing pitch.* Swelling increases the mass of your vocal cords. Increased mass gives you a lower-pitched voice.
- *Loss of high notes.* If your voice is usually able to reach high pitches and you can no longer hit those notes, that also could indicate swelling of your vocal folds. To reach a high note, the vocal folds must stretch thin, which they are less able to do when swollen.
- *Laryngeal pain.* Pain in your larynx is different than pain in your pharynx, which is something that we experience when we have an upper respiratory infection (sore throat). Pain in your pharynx, when accom-

panied by congestion, fever, or coughing, is a different phenomenon and is probably indicative of short-term swelling that is related to a virus or bacteria. A sore throat after using your voice extensively, in the absence of other symptoms of a cold, is a warning sign that you have probably overdone it and you need to rest your voice. Failure to rest your voice when you are experiencing pain can lead to injury.

- *Hoarseness.* Hoarseness, roughness, or scratchiness of the voice that isn't associated with being sick (or if it is associated with being sick, persists for more than a few days) can indicate that your vocal folds may be developing voice-related injury.

- *Breathiness or airiness.* This is the "Marilyn Monroe" sound of air leaking out around your vocal folds so that your voice has a whispered quality. Breathiness occurs when the vocal folds are not closing all the way due to swelling, tension, fatigue, or some other organic condition (neurological damage or lesions on the vocal folds). Whispering is an extreme version of breathiness.

- *Delayed onset of phonation.* When the very beginning part of a sound is breathy and it takes a moment for the voice to "kick in," this is referred to as "delayed onset." (Track 11 of the CD has an example of what this sounds like.)

- *Vocal fatigue.* Fatigue is a sensation in your throat that may not be strong enough to be considered "pain," but is still an *awareness* of your throat muscles. Any kind of negative sensation in your throat is a warning sign that you may be speaking in a way that is not ideal.

Managing Laryngitis

Many voice disorders originate from people "pushing through" an illness. When you are sick, especially if there is any kind of laryngitis associated with the illness, you should assume your vocal folds are swollen. Whenever the vocal folds are swollen, they are more vulnerable to injury. This is why it is important to allow the vocal folds to heal properly during and after an illness. Some people are able to continue their daily voice routine when they are sick. Others need to rest their voices completely in order to remain vocally healthy. Knowing your voice—its strengths as well as its limitations—will help you decide into which category you fall. See the Frequently Asked Questions at the end of the previous chapter for more information on talking when you are sick.

Wash your hands regularly to avoid illness.

Maintaining adequate hydration by drinking lots of water is all the more essential when you are sick. Inhaling steam and using a hot air humidifier in the bedroom are also especially helpful during illness. If you do talk when you are sick, most people find it helpful to use more breath. When the vocal folds are swollen, they are heavier, so it takes more air to make them move. Failure to provide adequate breath for swollen vocal folds to vibrate can result in strained speech, causing an increase in hoarseness. Also, avoid the temptation of letting your voice "sink into your throat." The feeling of "talking over" your throat is helpful when you are sick. In other words, use enough breath support and openness in the throat to create the sensation of the voice bypassing the throat.

Seeking Help

Knowing how and when to seek outside vocal help is just as important in avoiding long-term injury as is taking excellent care of your voice on a regular basis. In general, if you have hoarseness or any other negative change in your voice that lasts for more than four days in the absence of other symptoms of an illness (congestion, fever, vomiting, etc.) you may want to consider consulting an otolaryngologist (ear/nose/throat, or ENT, physician).

Hoarseness in relation to a cold is often treated by a primary care physician (PCP). Your PCP will most likely assess your throat by shining a light at the back of your mouth and looking at your tonsils and your pharynx. This procedure is adequate for looking for swelling or redness. However, when your PCP shines a light inside your mouth and holds your tongue down with a tongue depressor, she does not see your vocal folds at that moment. In order for your vocal folds to be seen and assessed, especially if hoarseness persists after the cold has resolved, it is recommended that you see an ENT physician.

As in all areas of medicine, otolaryngology has several subspecialties. We advise that you find an ENT physician in your area who specializes in voice care for professional voice users. We also recommend that you find an ENT physician who works closely with a voice-trained speech pathologist in a voice center.

The best method for vocal fold assessment is a procedure called *videostroboscopy* (video-strobe-OSS-kuh-pee). Videostroboscopy allows the ENT physician and the speech pathologist to see a highly magnified picture of your vocal folds vibrating in apparent slow motion. (See chapter 12 for a more complete explanation.) This allows them to examine not only the tissue integrity but also the movement patterns of the vocal folds. This exam reveals details of the vocal folds that are impossible to see without a strobe light. Some ENT clinics have the technology for this exam and others don't, so be sure to ask when you call to make an appointment whether or not you can expect to have videostroboscopy as part of your assessment.

Depending on the ENT's diagnosis, medication may be prescribed, further tests may be ordered, and voice therapy may be recommended. Voice therapy is used to treat most of the disorders caused by voice misuse, and is administered by a speech pathologist. As in the field of medicine, speech pathology has many subspecialties. Again, we feel it is important that you work with a speech pathologist who specializes in working with professional voice users.

Frequently Asked Questions about Preventing Vocal Injury

Q: *My voice gets tired when I talk in the car on road trips. Why?*

A: A moving vehicle has a surprising amount of background noise. If you have ever left the radio on when you get out of the car, you've probably noticed when you restart the engine that the radio is louder than it needs to be for a quiet environment. So, when you are talking in the car, it is especially important to be aware of using plenty of breath support, a relaxed throat, and forward vibration. Articulating well is also a good idea; you can get away with slightly less volume if you have really clear diction. Refer to chapter 11 for more information about speaking over background noise.

Q: *I find that my voice gets tired when I talk on the phone. Is there anything I can do about it?*

A: There are several aspects of talking on the phone that fool us into thinking that we don't need to use good voice techniques. If we cradle the phone with our shoulder, our alignment is compromised. And because the receiver of the phone is held so close to the mouth, phone users also often allow their resonance to slip back into their throat. Remember to always use adequate breath, alignment, and forward focus. Also, although cell phone technology is getting better, there are still many areas with poor reception where it is difficult for the other person to hear you, and during those times our natural tendency is to get louder. Because we don't want to yell at the person we are speaking to, we don't get loud with full breath support. If we get loud by squeezing the sound out, it causes strain and fatigue.

If you find that you are frequently asked to repeat yourself while using your cell phone, you may want to invest in a headset with noise-canceling technology. These headsets remove background noise, and some can even enhance your voice at the same time.

Q: Should I drink tea with honey and lemon if I am sick or hoarse?

A: It is believed that honey might have a soothing effect on the outer layer of the pharynx or the back of the throat. Inhaling the steam of a hot beverage may provide some additional moisture to the outer layer of the vocal folds as well. It is also true that the astringent nature of lemon may help in thinning of some excess secretions. So if you have an illness that is creating extra goo in the throat, then lemon might be useful. If you enjoy it, go right ahead! Remember to choose caffeine-free tea.

Q: Is my voice ruined if I get nodes?

A: The short answer is no. If you develop vocal nodules, it is important that you have therapy to rehabilitate your voice.

It is very common for vocal nodules to shrink to the point of irrelevance with therapy. The key is working with a speech pathologist who specializes in working with professional voice users. As with many health concerns, early identification of the problem is the key to a fast recovery.

Q: *When I am sick, it seems right to talk almost in a whisper just to protect my voice. Is that a good idea?*

A: As counterintuitive as it may seem, whispering not only does not protect the voice but in most cases is worse than talking normally. Most people produce a whispered sound by tensing the throat. Whispering, therefore, is not a good idea even when you are ill because it not only creates tension but is also likely to further dry out the vocal folds because of the amount of air that passes between them.

Even when you are sick (presuming that your voice is healthy enough to be doing any talking at all), it is usually ideal to speak with good breath support and good vocal fold closure. The main difference between voice use when you are sick and voice use when you are well is the amount you can withstand before reaching your limit and stopping. You still want support and resonance—though the recipe for achieving them changes when your vocal folds are swollen.

Avoid sprays that numb your throat. Pain is your body's way of saying, "Stop."

Q: *Is dairy bad for my voice? I have heard that it makes you phlegmy.*

A: Some people have lactose intolerance or dairy allergy. In those people, dairy can produce a thickening of the mucus that naturally lives in the throat. Other people, however, feel no effects from consuming dairy. So, if you feel like it makes you phlegmy, you are right, it does. If you feel like it doesn't make you phlegmy, then it doesn't. If you are one of those people with a phlegmy response to dairy then you may want to avoid it an hour or two before extensive or delicate voice use.

Q: *What do recreational drugs do to my voice?*

A: Anything you inhale into your lungs passes your vocal folds. Inhaled drugs such as cocaine are likely to leave small irritating particles on the vocal folds. Smoking marijuana also acts as an irritant. Just like cigarette smoke, marijuana smoke also delivers hot, dry air into an area that prefers moisture. Furthermore, marijuana is often not filtered.

There is no way to smoke that is not harmful to the voice. The further from the vocal folds the heat source is, however, the better. For those who insist on indulging, a vaporizer or a bong with an ice cube in it to cool the water is probably the least damaging of all the harmful ways of smoking. This does not address, however, the harmful effect of smoking on the respiratory system and the obvious negative impact this has on voice production. In addition, recreational drug use typically disrupts the body's sensory and motor mechanisms, which makes you more likely to engage in potentially damaging behaviors. The take-home message is that recreational drugs of any kind can be harmful to your voice.

11

Vocal Success: What to Do in Specific Situations and Environments

Professional and avocational voice users encounter a variety of speaking activities and challenges, and each situation requires a different approach for optimal performance. Everyone benefits from specific tips, exercises, and analysis of these situations. You will undoubtedly see yourself in one or more of the scenarios outlined in this chapter.

Speaking to Groups

The key to speaking successfully to groups of any size is engendering a sense of personal connection. People in the audience (be they around a conference table, in a lecture hall, or in a stadium) want to feel that you are speaking directly to them. The technical considerations of how to make that happen vary according to size of the group and room, but the principle is the same: speak clearly and from the heart. And do not underestimate the power of a smile!

Think of people whom you consider good speakers—what do they have in common? Typically, these people exude genuineness; we tend to be drawn to people who seem real and therefore trustworthy. Good speakers also seem to be truly interested in communicating with you, their listener. Even in televised seminars, these skilled speakers can create the feeling that they care about you receiving their message.

A challenge of speaking to groups is to remain natural in appearance while implementing the techniques required to get the job done. Think of it like an actor's performance: good actors appear to be natural and relaxed, but are constantly using techniques of one sort or another. Stage actors, for example, are aware of their blocking and where the light is, are projecting to be heard, and are subtly positioning themselves so the audience can see their faces even though they are supposed to be speaking to someone behind them on the stage. Film actors are aware of hitting their marks and are talking intimately with boom mikes inches from their faces. The ability to be aware of technique while appearing relaxed and natural is a skill unto itself that requires practice.

In addition to the technical suggestions outlined for various group sizes, any public speaker will benefit from working through the alignment, voice, breathing, resonance, and emphasis chapters in this book. Mastering that material allows you to speak in a free, genuine, authentic voice that can be adjusted easily to spaces and groups of any size.

Small (1 to 10)

The atmosphere in smaller groups is typically more casual than it is in larger presentations. That being said, the pressure of presenting at a board meeting can certainly be every bit as great as presenting to 100 people! If you are in a room that can hold significantly more people than are present, consolidate your audience so it feels more intimate. If possible, have everyone move to the front so that you are all in the same general space.

The first thing to consider is your body. Body language conveys a great deal of communicative information, and people make judgments based on it. Imagine a speaker whose shoulders are rolled forward and chest is slumped, who is looking down at her paper as she speaks. That speaker gives a particular impression, possibly of lack of confidence, lack of interest, lack of strength, or simply lack of skill. Now imagine a speaker with an open, comfortable posture who is engaging with you and your fellow listeners as she speaks. The impression is quite different.

Whether you are standing or sitting as you speak, you want to appear as comfortable as possible. Note that we didn't say you have to actually be as comfortable as possible—just to appear so! This is where it starts to become apparent why acting techniques are often used in public speaking training. Acting is not about feeling things but rather about making audiences feel things, and public speaking is a type of acting. While it would be ideal for you to actually be comfortable, it is not essential in order to be an effective speaker. There is a high degree of "fake it till you make it" involved. It is possible to be nervous and look cool.

In order to look comfortable, it is helpful to be physically relaxed. This will help you genuinely feel comfortable as well. Make sure your shoulder blades are releasing down your back so your shoulders aren't hunched up to your ears. Keep your chest lifted so it isn't collapsed and slumped, but without looking puffed-up and rigid. Keep your head aligned so your chin is level and you are looking straight ahead. If you are standing, keep your knees unlocked. When standing, it is also important to plant yourself to avoid pacing or fidgeting. Remember that such open body language generates a feeling of openness.

Whether you are seated or standing as you speak, aim to position yourself (and the group) so that everyone can see your face. There is a lot of communicative nuance on a speaker's face, so allow the audience to see yours. It is also easier to understand someone when we see his face, so if any members of the group have difficulty understanding you (because they have a hearing loss, or are not fluent in English, for example), it is easier for them if they can see your mouth as you talk.

The other reason to have your face visible is because it allows you to have eye contact with the people you are speaking to. Making eye contact is a vital aspect of speaking to groups. It keeps people engaged and creates a connection between the speaker and the listeners. You don't have to bounce your gaze around to a different person every three words, but you do want to get to everyone in the group. Make a point while looking at someone, then move on to someone else for the next point.

When speaking to a small group, especially in a small room, it is easy to forget to use any special vocal technique. But no matter how big or small the group may be, it is important to use your full, resonant voice. It not only makes it easy for people to hear you, it commands the space. Not that you want to yell or be overly loud, but keeping power in your voice is as important for talking to small groups as large groups. To that end, make sure you are breathing low and easily. For some people this is easier sitting, and for others it is easier standing. When you do your breathing exercises, do them in both positions so that you will be able to rely on the technique no matter what circumstances you are in. Breathing in this natural manner also causes your body to relax.

If you are speaking to children, it is helpful to add more vocal variety. The human ear seems to be attracted to change, and children in particular are drawn to variations in voice. If we consider "parent-ese" (the way caregivers speak to infants), we find that people intuitively use greater pitch range and vocal variety when speaking to babies. Most popular children's TV characters use greater dynamics and variety than do people speaking strictly to adults. Avoiding monotone and bumping up the vocal range will help hold children's attention.

Medium (10 to 40)

Speaking to medium-sized groups involves the same principles as speaking to small groups, with some additional considerations. We suggest you read the small group information before reading this section.

As with a small group, you want to control your space as much as possible. If possible, invite the audience to move to a centralized location. Aim to be positioned in a way that enables everyone to see your face. This suggestion may occasionally be ignored if context requires it. For instance, a trial lawyer might use specific movements and positions in the courtroom for maximal impact, and a teacher might read to a group of children lying down for nap time. But it works as a general rule.

Depending on the length of your talk and the configuration of the room, you may or may not be able to make eye contact with each person. Assuming you are not lit in such a way that precludes you from seeing the faces of the listeners, it is still important to make eye contact with them. If you don't get to every single person, don't worry about it. People feel you are connecting with them if they see you connecting with other audience members. If you make eye contact with someone as you make a point, then switch to someone else and so on, the audience understands on some level that you are speaking to them directly, even if you do not look at each individual. It is therefore more valuable to speak directly to one person at a time than to flit your gaze around the room, trying to make eye contact with everyone. Fewer deep connections are more powerful than a cursory glance at everyone in the room.

Speaking to a medium-sized group usually demands more energy from you than does speaking to a small group. Depending on the space, you might need to project your voice considerably. If you are not miked, you will certainly need to consider your vocal volume. You never want to give the impression of yelling or straining, but you want to use more vocal energy and loudness than one would typically use for everyday speech. When you project, use plenty of abdominal breath, keep your throat open and neck relaxed, and place your voice forward so it vibrates the bones of your skull. The resonance you learned in chapter 5 gives you power without having to yell or push.

Large (40+)

All of the considerations for small and medium groups apply here as well, so read through those sections before reading this one. The principles and goals are the same, but the way to get to them is a little different.

When speaking to a large group, you are unlikely to be able to make actual eye contact with many people. Much of the time you simply can't see their eyes because of lighting or their distance from you. However, you can use a theater technique called *spotting*. When actors do monologues, they choose a spot (probably at the back of the room) where they place the imaginary person they are talking to. They pretend to see someone there, and it feels to the audience as if they are talking to someone in particular. When speaking to a large group, you still can give the illusion of making eye contact by spotting. Pick a random point and deliver a piece of your message to that point, as though you were looking directly into someone's eyes. Then choose another point in a different part of the room to focus on for the next piece of your message. As with genuine eye contact, the aim is to appear to engage or connect, not simply to stare blankly. The people sitting where you happen to spot will absolutely feel that you are looking at and talking directly to them.

The larger the group, the greater the likelihood that you will be miked. If so, see the section below on making the most of your microphone. If you are not miked, however, it is more important than ever that you project your voice. In addition to using a loud, strong voice, you also want to pay attention to diction. People often confuse being able to hear someone with being able to understand them. It is possible to hear sounds but be unable to understand the words. Think of the often-parodied sound of announcements on a subway: a deafening, unintelligible mush.

Because of nerves or technical limitations, it is easy to seem stilted or rigid when speaking to a large group. One of the simplest ways to appear natural and relaxed is to smile. Even if people can't see your face, they can hear a smile in the voice. It tends to draw in the listener and give a feeling of warmth, safety, and ease. Not that we are suggesting you grin like a lunatic through an entire talk, but rather that you look for places where it would be natural and reasonable. Obvious places to smile include the beginning and end of your talk, as well as any "asides" or jokes you make.

If things don't run smoothly, be grateful for the opportunity to use mistakes to your advantage. Humorously acknowledging any technical glitches or other mishaps is a nice way to connect with the audience on a human level. It says, "We are in the same boat," and shows that you are present.

Adjusting for Room Acoustics

The type of space you are in can make a world of difference in how you use your voice. The size and shape of the room, the materials it was made with, and the contents of the room all play roles in making your job as a speaker easier or harder.

Room Size

Common sense suggests that we need to project more in a large space and less in a small one. While that is usually true, room size is not the only factor to consider, as you will see below. It is possible to speak quietly in a large space and still be heard. If you are speaking in an unfamiliar space, try to get into the space beforehand to get a feel for it. Have someone stand at the back and ask if they can hear and understand you easily as you talk. If you are unable to get into the room in advance, you can start your talk by asking if people can hear you in the back. A touring actor reported that when she went to a new theater, she would "breathe in the space": she would stand on the stage and take in a breath that she felt was sufficient to fill the space with sound when she used it to speak. If this image resonates for you, it can be a helpful guide. Give it a try the next time you talk in any kind of new space.

If you are speaking in a theater with a balcony, know that the best acoustics are up in the balcony. The worst acoustics are at the back of the auditorium underneath the balcony. If you want to test whether people can hear you, ask someone sitting under the overhang of the balcony. If you use your voice well (meaning you support with breath and use full resonance), you can be heard easily without a microphone in a well-designed theater.

Be careful not to "overblow" your space. Being louder than necessary can be tiring or damaging to you, and potentially annoying to your listener. Imagine hearing someone talk almost in a shout for an hour. Much more pleasant is the idea of hearing someone speak with an easy, warm resonance.

People and Objects in the Room

The contents of a room, as well as what those contents and the room itself are made of, affect its acoustics. Rooms that reflect sound are called *live spaces*, and rooms that soak up sound are called *dead spaces*. Fabrics, carpet, absorbent material, and bodies all absorb sound. Any room, therefore, is more acoustically dead when it is filled with people than when it is empty. If the floor is carpeted, or if the walls have fabric of any kind on them, these materials will soak up some of your sound before it can reach the ears of the audience.

Dead spaces require more vocal energy than live ones. The danger is the temptation to push. If we don't hear any of our own sound come back to us (in the form of reflected sound waves bouncing back to our ears), it is natural to talk louder. It is easy to push and strain from the throat in this condition. However, if you use good breath support, keep your throat open, and use good resonance, you will be able to be heard in even a dead space. Keep in mind that pushing from the throat is rarely as effective as opening the throat and using the techniques outlined in the earlier chapters.

Echo, Echo, Echo

Reflective surfaces and hard, nonporous materials in a room allow the sound waves to bounce around and make a room acoustically live. The good news is that it is easier to be heard in a live space, because the room amplifies your voice due to the reflection of sound waves off the hard materials. The bad news is that this reflection creates an echo, which can make it hard to be understood. The other bad news is that *all* sounds echo in a live room, so other noises will compete with your voice.

In a live space, be careful not to overproject. If you are louder than you need to be, it will be even harder to understand you. The most important consideration for working in an echoey space is diction. Because of the fuzzy nature of the reflected sound, consonants tend to get lost. In a live space, articulate with even more clarity and precision than you otherwise would (see chapter 7). When you are doing this well, you might even feel that you are overarticulating and being too conscious of your diction. The second important factor to consider is the rate of your speech. In a live space, you need to leave a little time for the sound to bounce around, so it is helpful to speak more slowly. If you speak too quickly, the sound waves run into each other, and it makes it harder for people to understand you. So allow a little space for the reflection.

Making the Most of Your Microphone

Microphone technique is often overlooked, and as a result many speakers are not getting all of the benefits they could out of being miked. The first thing to remember is that a mike doesn't make you clearer, just louder. In fact, the amplification of your sound causes a small reduction in clarity, so speaking with clear diction is at least as important with a microphone as it is without one. However, if the mike is close to your mouth, it could pick up little "pop" sounds from some of your consonants. There are many different kinds of mikes, and varying skill levels of the technicians who will help you use them. If possible, get a little practice with your mike so you know how it affects your speech.

Along those lines, it is also important to remember to let the mike do its job. If you are using a mike, you don't need to really project your voice; you can speak at a comfortable level. You do, of course, want to use good resonance so your voice is full and rich. But you don't need to yell, even if the large space makes it feel like you do. Speak in a comfortable voice when they set the mike level, and then remember it is there to help you.

If you have a lapel mike, be aware of where it is placed when you turn your head. If, for example, you are giving a slide presentation and expect to turn your head to the right frequently to reference your slides, put the mike on your right lapel. If possible, put it in the center of your body instead of on either side.

Managing Stage Fright

Stage fright is natural and inevitable. Preperformance jitters and nerves are commonplace even among the most seasoned speakers and performers. Stage fright is largely fueled by adrenaline, which can provide you with that "performance energy" that allows you to sparkle. The goal is not to banish the fear but rather to channel the nervous energy so that it is helpful instead of debilitating.

The single most effective tool for channeling your nerves is breathing. Breathing slowly, low and deep in the belly, helps to calm your body and mind. One reason is because deep breathing counteracts the "fight or flight" response and allows your muscles to relax and your heart rate to return to normal. Deep breathing also brings oxygen to your brain and muscles, helping you relax and center yourself. Another benefit of breathing deeply is that it gives your brain something to focus on other than being nervous! This is a meaningful benefit, because nervousness in your body is caused by the thoughts in your mind.

Redirecting the mind is a powerful tool for coping with fear and anxiety of all sorts, and stage fright is no exception. Most stage fright is based on questions like "What will they think of me?" and "How am I doing?" By focusing instead on your message—the content and how to communicate it clearly—the fear naturally diminishes because you stop feeding it. Telling yourself to stop being nervous is not always effective; it's hard to not do something. Focusing on your objective, however, gives you something useful to replace the nervous self-talk with.

Ever wonder what to do about dry mouth caused by nerves? Here are some suggestions: (1) Chew on your tongue to stimulate saliva. (2) Sip water during your presentation. (3) Eat something tart, like a green apple. (4) Think about a delicious food. (5) Hydrate well ahead of time.

Staying physically relaxed is another major stage fright buster. When we get nervous, our muscles tend to tense. We might fidget or sweat or get a dry mouth. If you consciously drop your shoulders, open your chest, unlock your knees, relax your hips, relax your hands, and take a deep breath, you will relax. And as we mentioned in a previous section, you can "fake it till you make it." If you relax the muscles of your body, your mind and body will think you are relaxed. If you are physically tense, your mind and body will think there is something to be tense about, and you are more likely to remain nervous. You also appear more confident if you are relaxed, and appearing confident can make you feel less nervous.

Finally, know that most people in the audience want you to do well. They are supportive of you. Being open to feeling the supportive, positive energy coming at you from the group can go a long way to allowing you to relax and enjoy the moment.

Pacing for Marathon Talking Days

Long days of continuous talking are difficult even for the most skilled vocalist. There is simply a physiological limit to how much strain the voice can take before it starts to complain. How much is "too much" varies by person, and knowing your own vocal limits is part of the process of your vocal education.

On days that will require a lot of talking over a long period, pace yourself. Imagine you have a vocal bank account with a finite amount of words in it, and be judicious about how you spend those words. If you have a say in the schedule, schedule breaks every 90 minutes or more often. Avoid talking during breaks and mealtimes if possible, don't make unessential phone calls, and generally limit your talking to only what you have to say to get the job done.

Sip water consistently and, if possible, schedule bathroom breaks to allow yourself to drink with impunity. Talking dries out the throat a bit, and constantly sipping water makes it more comfortable. Also, make sure you are not talking any louder than is necessary. When you do have a break, allow your voice to return to a quieter level.

The "anchor" introduced in chapter 5 is a useful tool for these marathon talking days as well. During breaks, use that exercise to help "reset" your voice. Producing sound with that strong forward vibration and no effort in the throat can be as good as, if not better than, voice rest. Gently humming with that forward placement seems to effectively massage your vocal folds and relax the other muscles of your throat.

Using the Telephone

The phone has become a ubiquitous accessory for many people, and many use it for the majority of their workday. Whether you use the phone for business or pleasure, the considerations are the same. The widespread use of earpieces and headsets is voice-friendly, because it removes a major mechanical consideration.

Cradling the phone between your ear and shoulder tends to create neck tension and alignment problems that encourage your voice to get stuck in the throat. Holding the phone in that kind of scrunched way can make it tiring to talk on the phone for long periods. Keeping your head aligned and posture solid remove that obstacle.

The other major factor that encourages people to use suboptimal vocal technique when talking on the phone is related to the psychology of the telephone itself. Because the other person's voice is right in your ear, and because you know that the mouthpiece of the phone is close to your mouth, it is easy to let the voice drop back into the throat. In short, we forget to use our vocal technique on the phone. Because it feels so intimate, and because we don't want to be too loud for the listener, it is common to use a low, throaty voice on the phone. The most important tip for talking on the phone is to use all the same techniques this book teaches for speaking in any other context. Using your full voice (as opposed to an unsupported, low-energy voice) will remove the fatigue factor that the telephone can generate.

If you are using a speakerphone, especially in a moving car, the best suggestion is to keep these calls brief or get an earpiece. A moving car has a tremendous amount of background noise that we don't typically notice. Couple that with the feeling of having to yell to be heard on a speakerphone, and you have a recipe for vocal fatigue and strain. Likewise, if you are talking to someone who is in a moving car, especially if they are on speaker, you can hear a lot of background noise over the phone line. It is tempting to push and yell to be heard over that noise (just as when your telephone partner whispers, you tend to get quieter as well).

If you use your breath support, alignment, and resonance, you can talk on the phone in a way that is no more difficult or tiring than talking to someone sitting next to you. Placing visual reminders in your environment can help you remember to use these techniques while on the phone. We usually recommend writing a reminder on a sticky note and putting it in your field of vision in the place where you use the phone most often. Some clients prefer to use random objects as reminders. For example, when they see a yo-yo on their desk and wonder why it's there, they remember to breathe.

Using Voice Recognition Software

Computer technology that allows you to dictate into the computer can be a mixed blessing. While it allows you to avoid typing, it can put a strain on the voice. The main vocal problems we have encountered when working with people using this equipment relate to pushing the voice. The software can be picky about what it registers, so people often feel the need to talk more forcefully than is really necessary. The software can also require people to speak a word at a time (as opposed to a thought or sentence at a time), which can cause more strain on the throat. Speak as easily and gently as the computer will allow, and use plenty of breath support.

An additional consideration has to do with pitch variety. It appears to us that people tend to get stuck in a monotone pitch range when using this software. Speaking in a small area of your pitch range can cause fatigue, so change it up. One reason this can be tiring has to do with repetitive strain. The vocal cords change length when we change pitch. When we speak at a single pitch, the muscles of the vocal folds don't get to change length, so they are working at the same length for a long period. This can possibly lead to a repetitive strain–type injury, which occurs when people do the same thing over and over with their muscles.

So use as much flow and variety as possible to keep your voice happy.

Speaking, Cheering, and Shouting Outdoors

Speaking outside, with or without amplification, presents a major vocal challenge. The main reason is acoustics—there are no walls to trap and reflect the sound. There are also other noises (cars, airplanes, trains, people, animals, and wind, to name a few) that you have to compete with.

Almost all outdoor speaking requires projection, so the next section on speaking over background noise will be useful for this situation as well. In addition to projecting your voice, it is essential to articulate very clearly in order to be understood outdoors. The sound gets lost so easily, even with amplification, that the strength of your consonants becomes more important than usual. The consonants help the listener to make sense of the possibly mushy sound that finally reaches their ears. Chapter 7 has exercises to help with this.

There is a particular "ring" that it is possible to find in the speaking voice. This ring is a combination of adequate breath support and shaping the mouth and throat to make the voice "pop"—to make it louder and more resonant. If you use the natural ability of your body to amplify sound (by finding this ring), you reduce the wear and tear on your throat. Realize that pushing your voice yields diminishing returns. Trying to push beyond your limits will make your voice thinner and quieter, despite your good intentions. Generally speaking, you want to create more open space in your throat instead of squeezing.

Keeping your voice in great shape is also essential if you do much outdoor speaking. Following the guidelines and precautions in chapter 10 to keep your voice as healthy as possible allows you to set yourself up for success rather than frustration.

Speaking Over Background Noise: Classrooms, Cars, and Bars

One of the most vocally challenging activities is talking over background noise. The principles for addressing this issue are the same whether the noise is coming from being in a moving vehicle, from a classroom full of little voices, or from the din of a nightclub. It is important to use good technique in these circumstances, because there is a real risk of damaging your voice (chapter 10 provides more information about this).

There are two basic approaches to talking over background noise. One approach is based on the fact that if we can't be louder than the noise in a room, it is helpful to be different than the noise. This technique is demonstrated on track 11of the CD, and it involves using a slightly higher pitch and a "twangy" sound. While this may sound peculiar in a quiet room, it is very useful in a loud environment. If you can use a different pitch or sound quality than the din, your voice will stand out and will be easier to hear. In addition to projecting your voice, it is helpful to articulate clearly when speaking over background noise. Even if people can't hear every sound, if the consonants are clear and your speech is easy to understand, they will get more of what you are saying. Chapter 7 will help you master this.

The "BE FAR" Method of Speaking Over Background Noise
- B: Breathe deeply before speaking
- E: Elevate the pitch of your voice just a bit
- F: Front—aim your voice to the front of your face
- A: Articulate your words with more vigor
- R: Relax your shoulders and neck

The second approach is to essentially shout. Shouting healthily involves breathing low and deep, using the abdominal muscles to send the air out, opening the throat to allow the acoustics of the vocal tract to amplify your voice, keeping your head aligned so you don't inadvertently close off your throat tube, thinking of "arcing" the sound out along the roof of your mouth, and keeping your pitch at a comfortable level (not too low). You want to avoid a feeling of the sound "catching" in your throat, and the tone should be clear (as opposed to rough or gravelly). You can learn how to use all of these elements in the chapters on breathing, alignment, and resonance.

Finally, remember that we can often control or adjust the environment more than we think. If you have to quiet a classroom, for instance, find a technique to do so that does not involve your voice (like flashing lights or ringing a bell). If you are out at a loud bar, get close to the people you are speaking to, perhaps talking right in their ears. Keep all these options in mind in order to protect your voice in loud environments.

Enhancing Your Vocal Image

Many people put a lot of energy into their physical image (hair, clothes, accessories, body shape, teeth, nails, etc.), yet often fail to consider their vocal image. The sound of your voice is a huge part of the general impression you make on people. Imagine a person whose vocal image is different from the image they otherwise project—like a hugely muscled boxer with a squeaky, high voice and a lisp. What sort of impression would that make?

One of our clients was a CEO in transition between jobs who was referred by an image coach because his vocal image did not match the image he was trying to project. He was a tall, strong-looking man, expensively dressed and well groomed, with a great resume, but his voice was twangy, nasal, and thin. Everything but his voice said "power." His voice said "weak." The incongruence between his voice and the rest of his image was jarring, and the image coach felt it could keep him from being taken as seriously as possible by potential employers. As he worked on releasing the physical tension and habits that led to his small voice, he found that the stronger, resonant voice felt more comfortable and natural. In addition to benefiting him professionally, he also felt better about his voice and vocal image on a personal level.

Confidence

We project confidence by appearing unafraid and relaxed. True confidence comes from a feeling of trust in our own abilities. Self-doubt and fear are the opposite of confidence. Therefore, being well prepared is a vital aspect of appearing confident. The more certain you are that you are going to say what you want to say, that you know what you are talking about, and that you can handle any challenging questions, the more confident you will appear. Taking that a step further, feeling you have a right to be there (wherever you are) on all levels makes you appear confident.

Confidence radiates from our eyes, our bodies, and our voices. The stereotype of someone who is lacking in confidence is someone looking down at the ground or nervously around the room, with rounded shoulders and a collapsed chest, or fidgeting, speaking in a small, uncertain voice. The opposite of that constellation of behaviors, then, gives the impression of confidence: solid eye contact, open and relaxed body language, and a strong, free voice.

Unapologetic eye contact goes a long way to projecting confidence. Friendly, engaged connection with whomever you are speaking to shows that you are not afraid. When we are afraid, nervous, or experiencing self-doubt, we tend not to look people in the eye. Perhaps this is related to the adage about eyes being the window to the soul. If we are hiding something (like our fear or self-doubt), we don't want to open the shades so people can see in that window!

Feeling at home in your skin—or at least appearing to feel that way—makes you appear confident. Fidgeting or picking at a piece of paper suggests that you are not feeling comfortable and relaxed. Likewise, allowing your shoulders to roll forward and your chest to collapse gives an impression of hiding or holding back. The other extreme of a puffed-out chest and rigidly opened shoulders, however, can also give an impression of tension. Moving your shoulder blades down your back and keeping your shoulders relaxed, breathing low and deep from the abdomen, and keeping your spine straight but fluid, makes your body appear relaxed and confident. The alignment and breathing chapters provide more specific information about how to attain this state.

Easy, deep breathing not only relaxes you, but is also a key ingredient to the strong voice that usually accompanies confidence. Note that we did not say "loud" voice—many people attempt to simulate confidence by being overly loud, which only serves to make them appear to be trying too hard, which is not consistent with confidence. The resonance chapter teaches you to find your natural, free, powerful, radiating voice. That full, rich sound requires a lack of tension in the throat, and lack of tension is one of the hallmarks of confidence. On some level, people know your voice is open and relaxed, which makes you appear confident.

Charisma

Charisma is difficult to define, but for our purposes is related to charm. It's a quality that draws people in and makes them want to be around you. One attribute people often enjoy in someone is an appearance of happiness. Charismatic people tend to put out what can best be described as "a good vibe." These people tend to be pleasant and upbeat. They radiate positive energy, and people want to be around it.

On a physical level, one of the main ways we radiate energy is through the eyes and face. Charismatic people usually have bright, sparkly eyes—even if they are not feeling genuinely happy, they appear to be so. They have an easy, genuine smile (not to be confused with a fake smile plastered on the face) and pleasant demeanor. Their facial expressions are usually open and positive.

Becoming aware of your facial expressions can be helpful in cultivating your innate charisma. Do people ever ask you why you are frowning, when you were not meaning to frown? Many of us carry habitual tension in our facial muscles that can make us appear to scowl or frown when we are just concentrating or feeling neutral. Other people are often told they are hard to read, because their faces belie so little information that they appear masklike. Knowing your own "facial baseline" (by observing your facial expressions and by using the exercises in the alignment and warm-up chapters) will help you gain control of the impression you make on others.

From a vocal perspective, people with charisma tend to use a lot of vocal variety and range. This adds to the impression they give of being interested and excited in life in general, and in their audience in particular. Vocal range and variety are also hallmarks of enthusiasm, confidence, and expressivity. Chapters 5, 6, and 9 provide specific exercises to help you add more variety to your voice.

And while not obviously related to voice—perhaps it is the other side of the coin—charismatic people are often good listeners as well. They don't feel the need to take up more auditory space than is necessary. Listening makes them appear interested in other people, which is part of the charisma.

Power

Power can refer to the ability to do something, such as the power of locomotion. It can also refer to one's influence or control over people or outcomes. In this context, however, we are referring to power in the more holistic sense of projecting an aura of strength.

If you have not done so already, read the above section on confidence. A key element of projecting an aura of strength is confidence. Everything discussed there is relevant to this topic as well. Low, centered breathing and a strong, open body position go a long way to giving the impression of power. Unapologetically taking up space and meeting people's gaze with strong eye contact are important as well.

As Americans, we often equate power with size. While this does not mean that you need to gain 20 pounds or wear lifts in your shoes, it does explain why the idea of a bigger voice and presence might help you appear more powerful. A powerful voice is not breathy (airy, whispery) or constricted (squeezed, tight). It is resonant and full. The chapters on resonance and vocal warm-up will help you find this aspect of your own voice.

A powerful voice also tends to have a rich, deep tone, but many people we have worked with as voice clinicians have gotten themselves into trouble by artificially trying to lower the pitch of their voices to sound stronger or more powerful. While you don't want to be talking in too high a pitch, there is a limit to how low you can bring your voice without doing damage to it. What can make the voice sound lower in a healthy way is using lower resonators. When your throat is tight and closed-in, your voice shoots up into the higher resonators (your cheekbones and head). This can lead to a shrill or high sound. When the throat is very open and relaxed, the voice can drop into the lower resonators (the front-of-face and chest) without having to artificially lower the pitch. Exercises designed to help you open the throat are Rest Position in chapter 2 and Warm-Up Exercises, Part I, in chapter 9.

Approachability

Approachable people are usually warm and friendly, and they make others feel comfortable around them. Body language is a big factor in how open and warm someone appears. The chapter on alignment provides specific information and exercises to help you become aware of any postural issues you may have and change them. Because approachable people are easy to talk to, they are also usually good listeners. They give the sense that they are happy to be talking to you by focusing on you and not appearing distracted. They often appear to "drop everything" to turn their attention toward you. Friendly eye contact and an easy smile go a long way toward giving the impression of approachability.

If you want to be perceived as approachable, let the word "open" be your mantra. Think of opening your energy, your heart, and your voice to whomever crosses your path. An open voice comes from literally opening the pathway for voice and supporting the sound with breath. Abdominal breathing and an open, unconstricted throat help achieve this sound. The chapters on breathing, resonance, and warm-up offer material toward this end. Approachable people also usually seem genuine and non-threatening. The section below discusses this concept in more depth.

Trustworthiness

Trustworthy people give the impression of being honest and reliable. It's interesting that two common expressions about trustworthiness involve speech. We "tell" the truth and we keep our "word," even though the latter refers more to following through on actions. We keep our word by doing what we say we will do; the doing is essential, but it begins with the promise of the word.

We tend to trust people who are genuine and authentic. People who appear transparent, not to be hiding anything, seem trustworthy. If we consider someone who seems the opposite of trustworthy, we conjure up someone like the stereotypic shifty used car salesman, who seems fake and gives the impression that he has something to hide (for instance, because he can't make eye contact), or someone who is a "flake" (unfocused, flighty, or forgetful). Therefore, the information about relaxed and comfortable physicality and eye contact discussed in the section on confidence is equally relevant here.

A free and natural voice gives the impression of genuineness because it is organic. Many people have tension in the voice, which they may or may not be aware of, that can cause them to sound artificial. Working through the chapters on breathing, alignment, and resonance will help you find your own strong, natural voice. To be perceived as trustworthy, be aware of your word—i.e., what you say and what you promise—and follow through with your actions.

If you desire more help with your vocal image after working through the book, remember that there are voice coaches out there who can help you. (Resources are available in the appendix.)

12

Behind the Scenes: Additional Technical Information

This chapter is intended for voice trainers, voice enthusiasts, and anyone interested in additional technical information about voice production. While we include some information about the anatomy and physiology of voice production in the other chapters, we limit it so as to avoid overwhelming people who do not need (or care about!) the details. In this chapter we provide additional information that we share with some of our clients, specifically those who either need it to understand the material or who simply find it interesting.

We find that the common thread that unifies the seemingly disparate aspects of speech production (anatomy and physiology of the respiratory and phonatory systems as well as acoustic principles) is alignment. The relationship of these subsystems, and the relevance of their function, is demonstrated through the affect that alignment (or misalignment, as the case may be) has on them and therefore on voice. So throughout the chapter we will draw your attention to the relationship of alignment to anatomy and physiology.

In addition to the additional information about mechanics, anatomy, and physiology, we also include some information for voice coaches about working with students with medical issues affecting voice as well as students who are hoarse. Finally, we include information about basic instrumentation for voice analysis used in voice centers.

Breathing Basics

Your lungs are two pear-shaped structures located within your thorax (figure 12-1). The *thorax* is your chest cavity, and it basically forms a box around your lungs. The ceiling of this box is made up of the shoulders and *clavicles* (collarbones). The front, side, and back walls of the box are the *sternum* (breast bone), ribs, and spine. The ribs attach to the spine in the back and wrap around the body. The upper ribs attach via cartilage to the sternum in the front. The lower ribs attach by a cartilage to the cartilage of the ribs above them instead of attaching to the breastbone.

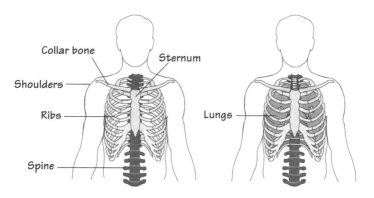

Figure 12-1: Thorax and breathing anatomy

The lowest ribs are called the "floating ribs" because they don't attach to anything in the front. Cartilage is more flexible than bone, so this design suggests that the lower rib cage is more flexible than the upper because it has more cartilage and less bone.

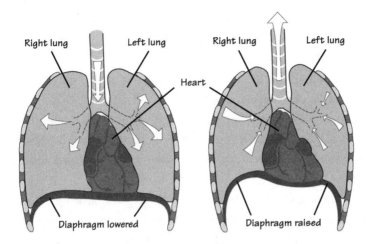

Figure 12-2: Diaphragm flattens as you breathe in.

Figure 12-3: Diaphragm raises when you breathe out.

The lower lungs are larger than the upper lungs. When the lungs expand, they inflate primarily in a downward direction as opposed to an upward direction. The floor of the thorax is the diaphragm muscle. The diaphragm is actually located at the bottom of your rib cage (there is a common misconception that it located much lower). When you inhale, your thorax has to get bigger in order to make room for the lungs to expand. To accomplish this, the diaphragm contracts and flattens, lowering the floor of the thorax. The *external intercostals* (one set of muscles between the ribs) also contract to expand the rib cage. Because the thorax is made larger, the pressure inside is now lower than the air pressure outside. As a result, a vacuum is created inside the thorax that sucks air into the lungs (figure 12-2).

When the diaphragm flattens, it also pushes downward on the internal organs in the abdominal cavity. The organs, which are packed together tightly, are displaced. Because the abdominal wall (belly) has the most flexibility, it moves outward to make room for the displaced organs. This action accounts for the feeling of breathing "into" the belly. The abdomen doesn't literally fill with air, but rather is moving outward to make room for the innards that are pushed downward by the flattening diaphragm. While the back muscles have less give than the abdominals because they are stabilizing us, they also move outward (though not as far) in the area between the bottom of the rib cage and the hips.

When you exhale, the diaphragm releases back up into its dome shape, which raises the floor of the thorax back up. The external intercostals (which have lifted the lower rib cage out to the sides) release, allowing the rib cage to relax. At the same time, the *internal intercostals* (the other set of muscles between the ribs) contract to pull the rib cage in even further, making the thorax even smaller. These actions, along with the resulting pressure shift, cause air to flow out of the lungs (figure 12-3).

Breathing and Alignment

As you can imagine, breathing for speech is at its best when one's alignment facilitates full and dynamic movement of the rib cage and diaphragm to accommodate the expansion and deflation of lung tissue. Therefore, when optimizing alignment to benefit the respiratory subsystem of speech and singing, we look to align and release shoulders, to keep the spine straight, and to release the belly to facilitate diaphragmatic contraction. A stance involving unlocked knees and the feet under the hips is believed to place the pelvis in a position to optimize diaphragmatic expansion as well. Conversely, a *mis*aligned body—slumped shoulders, rounded back—prevents the respiratory system from functioning well.

More Interesting Facts about Vocal Cord Vibration

As we explained in chapter 4, when we produce voice, the vocal folds are brought together and air is exhaled through them, causing them to vibrate. Taking a closer look, we first see air pressure building up underneath closed vocal folds. When the air pressure gets to a certain point, the vocal folds are blown apart. Then the air that has just blown the folds apart now sucks them back together. This is called the *Bernoulli Effect*. This principle also accounts for the fact that a person on the side of the road being passed by a fast-moving truck gets pulled toward the truck rather than pushed away from it. When air moves quickly between two things, it pulls them together. Therefore, the air moving through the vocal folds causes them first to open and then to close. Vocal fold vibration will stop if (1) there is insufficient air pressure to "blow" the vocal folds apart, (2) the vocal folds are not close enough to each other (i.e., are in a V position), or (3) the vocal folds are closed too tightly, prohibiting air to "blow" them apart and initiate vibration.

Most of the characteristics of vocal fold vibration depend on the position of the vocal folds themselves as determined by the contraction and relaxation of the intrinsic laryngeal muscles (*intrinsic* means that the muscle is entirely contained within the larynx). Keep in mind that both sides of the larynx are mirrors of each other, so each intrinsic muscle has a twin on the other side of the larynx. The basic intrinsic laryngeal muscles include the vocal folds themselves (thyroarytenoids), the muscles between the arytenoids (interarytenoids), a pair of muscles that run from the cricoid to the thyroid (cricothyroid), a pair that run from the back of the cricoid up to the arytenoids (posterior cricoarytenoid), and a pair that run from the sides of the cricoid up to the arytenoids (lateral cricoarytenoid). Vibration frequency and intensity are influenced by the coordinated contraction and release of these muscle groups. Three of the intrinsic muscles act to bring the vocal folds together, creating an I shape to the larynx when looking at it from above. These are the interarytenoids, the thyroarytenoids, and the posterior cricoarytenoids. The only intrinsic laryngeal muscle that opens the vocal folds into a V shape is the lateral cricoarytenoid. Vocal fold elongation (which raises pitch) is achieved when the cricothyroid contracts.

The vocal folds themselves are made up of muscle covered by four layers of increasingly gelatinous tissue (figure 12-4). The deepest part of the vocal folds is muscle (thyroarytenoid). The next layer has a lot of *collagen* fibers, which are like thread. The layer beyond that is comprised of fewer collagen fibers and more *elastin* fibers, which are like rubber bands. The next layer toward the surface is made up of very gelatinous material and cells; this layer vibrates readily due to its "floppiness." The outermost layer is *epithelial tissue*, which is like the lining of the inside of the cheek. The epithelial tissue holds the whole thing in place. The vibration of the vocal folds is, in large part, a vibration of the epithelium and the gelatinous layers overlying the vocal fold muscle.

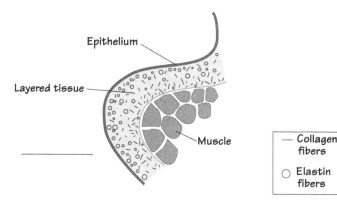

Figure 12-4: Layers of the vocal folds

Vocal fold vibration is passive, like a flag in the wind. The stiffer they are, the harder it is for them to vibrate.

The repetition of the vocal folds coming apart and being sucked together happens at an extremely fast rate. In fact, the average rate of vibration for females is approximately 200 Hz, which means 200 cycles per second. In other words, for every second a female is using her speaking voice, the vocal folds come apart and are sucked back together about 200 times. For adult males the rate is around 100 times per second. The higher the pitch of the voice, the greater the number of times the vocal folds vibrate. The human voice typically can produce sound as high as 1,500 Hz (high soprano) and as low as 70 Hz (low bass).

There are three main determinants of how many cycles per second the vocal folds vibrate. One is how massive they are. More massive vocal folds naturally vibrate slower, creating lower frequencies. That's one of the reasons that female voices generally sound higher than male voices—women's vocal folds are smaller and therefore vibrate faster.

Another is how much air pressure is built up underneath them. In general, the greater the air pressure, the faster the vocal folds naturally want to vibrate. This is why people's voices tend to go up in pitch when they get louder. Increasing airflow is one of the ways we increase loudness, so we have to override the body's natural tendency to raise pitch with increased air pressure.

The last is how stiff the vocal folds are at that moment. They vibrate faster (and therefore create a high pitch) when they are stiffer, thinner, and longer. Elongating the vocal folds increases their stiffness. To elongate the vocal folds, the cricothyroids contract, causing the front of the thyroid cartilage to tilt forward and down toward the cricoid. This tilt temporarily increases the distance between the tip of the thyroid cartilage and the arytenoids. As a result, the vocal folds, which run from the thyroid to the arytenoids, stretch out, making them stiffer and decreasing the amount of mass that vibrates. The result is a higher vocal pitch. Conversely, shortening the vocal folds and thereby making them fatter increases their vibrating mass and decreases their stiffness. This lowers pitch because the vocal folds vibrate more slowly.

> Musical notes are defined by frequency of vibration. Middle C is 262 cycles per second, regardless of whether it is made by a male voice, female voice, or musical instrument.

The larynx also has several extrinsic laryngeal muscles. These muscles are attached on one end to the larynx and on the other end outside the larynx. Extrinsic laryngeal muscles run from the larynx to the jaw, tongue, head, sternum, collar bone, and shoulders. There are also ligaments which bind the larynx to other neighboring structures.

The Larynx and Alignment

By encouraging release and relaxation of the shoulders, jaw, tongue, back of the neck, and upper chest, we also decrease rigidity of the larynx. This allows it to move as needed to achieve the vocal task at hand. Correct alignment also encourages a straight back of neck and a slightly tucked chin to overcome a chin jut position. There are two main vocal reasons for overcoming a chin jut position. One is to further facilitate an untethered larynx; the other is to benefit the resonatory subsystem of speech. To better understand the benefits for the larynx, refer to figure 12-5.

Here you will see several muscles and ligaments of the neck. Draw your attention to the stylohyoid ligament. This ligament runs from the styloid process behind the ear down to the hyoid bone, which is the top-most structure of the larynx. Our goal with alignment is to keep that ligament in a neutral position, which are achieved when the ears are basically over the shoulders. A chin jut posture lengthens the distance between the styloid process and the hyoid bone.

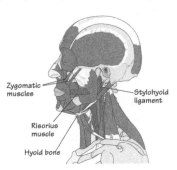

Figure 12-5: Face and neck muscles

Because it is a "floating bone," meaning that it is held in place by soft tissue attachments, the hyoid bone and, therefore, the larynx are likely to rise up slightly when the stylohyoid ligament is pulled during chin jut. When optimizing vocal production for speech and singing, a high larynx caused by mechanical upward yanking from the stylohyoid ligament due to misalignment of the head is certainly not what we are looking for.

To clarify, the larynx does appropriately venture upward in some types of singing and vocalizing. It is not the high larynx itself that is problematic, but rather the way in which it is elevated. Raising the larynx using muscles can be fine; pulling it up because of misalignment is not. A chronically high larynx can cause discomfort and fatigue as well as impose a "pinched" vocal resonance.

Crash Course on Vocal Acoustics

It is useful to know a few acoustic principles to understand vocal resonance with more depth.

Overtones

Every tone that we produce has a *fundamental frequency* (usually the pitch that we hear—it is determined by the number of times per second the vocal folds vibrate), and overtones, which are essentially shadow tones of that fundamental. *Overtones* (also known as *harmonics* or *partials*) are components of a sound that we usually can't hear individually. The overtones are multiples of the fundamental; that is, if the fundamental frequency is 200 Hz, the overtones occur at 400 Hz, 600 Hz, 800 Hz, and so on. The composite of a fundamental frequency and overtones is heard as a single pitch. Interestingly, some musical traditions include overtone singing (such as Tuvan singers), which involves shaping the vocal tract so that individual overtones can be distinguished by the human ear.

Resonant Frequency

If you tap a glass, it vibrates at a particular frequency and actually produces a tone that we can hear. If you hit a table, there is a certain speed at which it vibrates. An object's *resonant frequency* is the frequency at which it vibrates the most strongly. The vocal tract also has a resonant frequency. (Actually, the vocal tract has several resonant frequencies because it is made up of a series of tubes capable of changing size and shape independent of each other and, therefore, affecting resonant frequency in a multitude of ways. Because this concept makes most people's heads spin, however, we are simplifying the vocal tract to a single tube for the purpose of discussion in this chapter.)

Differently sized and shaped tubes have different resonant frequencies. When you change the size or shape of the vocal tract, you change its resonant frequency. A larger tube has a lower resonant frequency, and a smaller tube has a higher resonant frequency. That is because the resonant frequency is determined by the amount of time it takes an air molecule to go all the way to one end of the tube and back. Notice that if you fill a bottle with water at the sink, the tone you hear gets higher as the bottle gets fuller. That's because the remaining space in the bottle (the tube in this analogy) gets smaller as the water takes up increasingly more space.

Selective Amplification and Reinforcement

When you sound a complex tone (such as voice) through a tube (such as the vocal tract), the tube will amplify and reinforce (make louder to the ear) the overtones that are closest to its own resonant frequency. So a *larger* tube (which has a *lower* resonant frequency) will amplify the lower *overtones*. This makes the voice sound relatively low. A smaller tube (with a higher resonant frequency) amplifies the higher overtones, making the voice sound relatively high.

Formants

A *formant* is a resonance of the vocal tract. This is essentially a cluster of sound waves at a particular frequency, which is determined by the size and shape of the vocal tract. Remember that changing the shape of a tube changes its resonant frequency.

Well, the throat is a series of tubes that can create many different shapes. With each shape, the tube has a particular resonant frequency. Sound energy becomes concentrated around these particular frequencies, or formants. Our ear can discern formants more easily than it can hear individual harmonics, because formants contain a lot of acoustic energy. In fact, vowels are determined and identified by their two lowest formants. The sounds *eee* and *ah* are different from each other because the shape of the vocal tract (tube) is different. Creating the open tube for *ah* (with a low tongue and relatively open jaw) creates particular formants that we can identify. Similarly, the small tube created when we raise the tongue to say *eee* has its own formants that we can perceive. Certain formants can be useful to a speaker or singer. The "singer's formant" is a peak of harmonic energy around 2,000 to 3,000 Hz that can help operatic singers project over an orchestra, and is perceived as "ring" in the voice. There is also indication of a "speaker's formant" in trained speakers, most commonly actors.

Acoustics and Alignment

The take-home point here is this: the bigger the tube, the lower, deeper, and richer the voice will sound. Achieving a big vocal tract (one that isn't constricted through excessive tension) is our target. We're not intending to stretch the vocal tract for daily use, but rather to avoid making it smaller by inadvertently constricting it. Voice trainers and therapists are on the lookout for any type of chronic tension that occurs in the face, neck, and shoulders which may be constricting and shortening the vocal tract. Misalignment of the head distorts the shape of the vocal tract, narrowing the diameter and creating the effect of a higher pitch.

Contraction of the "smile" muscles also affects the acoustics of the vocal tract. Revisit figure 12-5: the *zygomatic muscles* run from the corners of the mouth up to the cheekbone, and the *risorius muscles* run from the corners of the mouth straight back. Many people unwittingly carry chronic tension in these muscles, which shortens the vocal tract and can reduce resonance.

Working with Students Who Have Medical Complications

We are going to briefly describe a few common medical complications that, when they occur, necessitate a team approach to achieve comfortable, accessible, and functional voicing. While we have no intention of delving into the medical pathophysiology of these disorders, we focus on the effect they have on the voice and the resultant need for referrals.

Asthma

According to the 2005 Summary Health Statistics for U.S. Adults and the 2006 Summary Health Statistics for Children, approximately 15.7 million adults and 6.8 million children in the U.S. suffer from asthma, a condition that causes constriction of the bronchi. Asthma is typically controlled by using inhaled corticosteroids which dilate the bronchi. Asthmatics may have developed compensatory tensions within their respiratory systems after years of difficult breathing. These tension-based mechanisms are often counterproductive and should be addressed. Additionally, the amount of breath needed to vibrate their vocal folds (which is called the *phonation threshold pressure*) can be more effortful to create and maintain. As a result, this population is at risk for clenching of the muscles that bring the vocal folds together and hold them there.

When working with this population, we assume that a pulmonologist is already on "the team," but if not, the vocalist will want to enlist one. Teachers must keep in mind the risk of laryngeal strain for untreated or undertreated asthmatics. Additionally, phrase lengths may be necessarily shorter due to lack of exhalatory power. Helping a student compensate by taking more frequent and deeper breaths can assist in decreasing laryngeal tension.

Many students with asthma are so accustomed to having breathing difficulties that they may exhibit some resistance to breath work on the grounds that they don't believe it will work for them. It can be helpful to explain to such students that asthma symptoms can be like an iceberg. Only a small fraction of an iceberg is visible above the water, with the majority underneath. For many (though obviously not all) students with asthma, the asthma itself often represents the proverbial tip of the iceberg (the portion that is visible). The rest of the symptoms (the hidden bulk of the iceberg) can be caused by the *compensation* for the actual illness. In other words, when a person feels they can't breathe, it is completely natural to get tense. Thus, many people with asthma inadvertently hold chronic tension in their breathing muscles. While this is an understandable response to bronchial constriction, it is not necessary. Breath work might not help the asthma itself; it can, however, help the asthma symptoms, many of which are caused by compensatory muscular tension.

Last, a note on inhalers. As of the printing of this book, a definitive link between certain inhalers and hoarseness or laryngeal changes has not been conclusively proven. There is, however, a common belief among many voice therapists and otolaryngologists that inhalers irritate the vocal folds. According to preliminary data, it appears that long-term use of corticosteroids can cause bowing of the vocal folds, making it harder for them to touch each other during vibration. Students should consult a pulmonologist if they experience a shift in vocal quality or overt dryness in the mouth and throat. There may be alternative medications that can be prescribed. To minimize the negative vocal side effects of inhaler use, it is recommended that asthmatics use a spacer with their inhalers and that they swish, gargle, and spit plenty of water after inhaling corticosteroids.

Paradoxical Vocal Fold Movement

There exists a laryngeal phenomenon in which the vocal cords come together when a person inhales, thereby closing the airway. Historically, there have been many names for this disorder including, but not limited to, fictitious asthma, vocal cord dysfunction, and paradoxical vocal fold movement (PVFM). When the vocal folds close during inhalation they may vibrate, creating a high pitched, wheezelike sound. The sound, together with the obvious struggle to breathe, is quite alarming for the person suffering from PVFM as well as for the witnesses of such an episode of respiratory distress.

Often PVFM episodes are triggered by exercise; this seems to occur more often in females than in males. Additionally, adolescent athletes are in a high-risk group for PVFM. While physician awareness of this condition is on the rise, it continues to be misdiagnosed as exercise-induced asthma and therefore mistreated. The evaluation for PVFM is relatively simple and includes observing laryngeal behavior during an episode of respiratory distress. The treatment is speech therapy with a voice specialist, which is basically laryngeal and respiratory control therapy. Some of the respiratory and alignment goals to optimize voice production are also strategies to remediate PVFM. In addition to establishing an action plan for when an episode occurs, individuals with PVFM are also trained to use the muscles of the respiratory and phonatory systems in such a way that they can open the airway when it closes.

If your voice student has asthma and does not seem to be improving with medication, he may need a work-up for PVFM.

As a vocal coach or teacher, it is entirely appropriate for you to gain permission to discuss your students' respiratory health with their pulmonologist, and we encourage you to do so.

Acid Reflux

The material in this section builds on the introduction to the topic of acid reflux provided in chapter 10. Acid reflux is becoming ubiquitous in our society. In short, reflux occurs when stomach juices return up the esophagus and sometimes repeat into the throat, mouth, and nose. Gastroesophageal reflux disease (GERD) causes acid to repeat back up into the esophagus, usually causing heartburn. Laryngopharyngeal reflux (LPR) specifically refers to the type of reflux wherein refluxant bathes the larynx and pharynx. A full understanding of the damage reflux can cause has yet to be achieved. Hypotheses exist that link reflux with as serious a disease as laryngeal cancer. More widely accepted, however, is a link between LPR and hoarseness, phlegm, and globus sensation (a feeling of a lump in the throat). Some studies suggest that about 50 percent of people with voice disorders also have LPR.

If your voice student is complaining of these symptoms, you will want to suggest that they be seen by an ENT physician or a gastroenterologist to rule out LPR. Encourage your student to seek out an ENT physician with a specialty in voice disorders. LPR cannot be ruled out using the conventional diagnostic tools used to evaluate GERD. The gold standard as of now is called a double pH probe. This is a thin wire with two sensors on it. The wire is inserted through the nostril and passed down into the esophagus. The two sensors are located at the top and bottom of the esophagus. The probe is worn for 24 hours, during which time acidity levels are detected by the sensors and reported on a monitor. As a voice trainer, your goal is to encourage your student to get help. Long-term exposure to refluxant appears to compromise the tissues of the larynx and can prevent vocal improvement and cause hoarseness.

Anxiety

The relationship between voice and anxiety is complex. Clinically anxious voice students can present additional challenges when releasing tensions and finding courage to explore the voice. Even students with "everyday" stress and anxiety can inadvertently carry tension in their throats and respiratory systems. Also, students who have been diagnosed with vocal issues can become anxious as they cope with their disorders.

The nuance of vocal quality can carry subtle information about the personality, meaning, and intention behind a speaker's words. We often make assumptions about someone's emotional state from vocal tone, even when the speaker may be trying to hide her inner state of being from her listener. The voice, inarguably, is an integral part of a person's identity and often holds the burden of communicating with, thereby connecting with, all other beings in that person's environment. It is not much of a jump to tie anxiety to laryngeal tension. Basically, when someone sounds tense, they usually *are* tense. In some cases, individuals can be so tense that they create a chronic state of hoarseness or complete voice loss during or after a life crisis.

As a vocal coach, you are likely to confront everyday anxiety and stress in your students. When working with a voice housed in a tense environment, it is of the utmost importance to relieve as much extraneous tension as possible before voicing. This sounds so very basic, but it never ceases to amaze us how many choir directors forgo relaxation exercises of the neck and face before vocalizing with their choirs. Common low-level stress and anxiety resulting in laryngeal, jaw, neck, and shoulder tension must be addressed in a vocal studio. Some students may benefit from yoga-type stretching and relaxation, while others may need progressive relaxation and meditation. Some may need a referral to a counselor for stress management strategies or medication. Other red flags to look for before suggesting a referral to a counselor include panic attacks, suicidal thoughts, chronic depression, poor sleep habits (insomnia, or inability to get out of bed in the morning), or changes in eating habits. Usually you can simply ask your student to report any of these issues to their primary care physician. At that point, the doctor will initiate the referral process to the appropriate professionals.

If a person has been diagnosed with a voice disorder, he may feel quite unstable. It is possible that he may grieve the loss of not only vocal health but also the sense of vocal invincibility. He may feel anxious as he looks ahead to his vocal commitments and grapples with keeping them while also healing the vocal folds. Self-confidence can falter a bit as a vocalist discovers that he needs to adjust his vocal habits. Denial is always possible. By providing support, understanding, and flexibility for your student during this difficult time, you can be an integral part of his healing process.

For many performers, identity and psyche are linked to voice. Asking a performer to change her voice can be tantamount to asking her to change her personality. Similarly, conveying that an individual has abused her voice, thereby causing vocal damage, can destabilize the psyche and trigger sensations of guilt and self-doubt. The connotation of the phrase "vocal abuse" is destructive and should therefore be avoided. Sometimes vocal damage occurs because of genetic predisposition to it. It is unhelpful and often not entirely accurate to pin vocal damage solely on poor singing or speaking technique, poor vocal hygiene, or vocal overuse or abuse. A more sensitive approach is to help a student understand that each person has her own limits of voicing before lesions are created. Healing those lesions involves learning how to modify vocal use and vocal hygiene to stay below the threshold of injury. Reframing in this way can help the student avoid unnecessary feelings of guilt and self-loathing, both of which can impair self-efficacy.

Once in voice therapy, students are asked to change vocal hygiene behaviors as well as speaking habits. This process can be time-consuming and daunting at first for some people. Some students feel they lack the ability to make the required changes. Others insist that their schedules are too busy. Usually these self-imposed roadblocks to healing are rooted in deeper issues such as denial, self-sabotage, or lack of trust in caregivers.

Fear is also a common emotion for students with medical problems. Vocal fold surgery is often misperceived as both inevitable and risky. The truth is, most cases of hoarseness can be treated without surgery, even when lesions are present. Education is the first line of defense against students' fears. Once informed, students are reassured, and their anxieties are managed with specific self-help directives empowering them to heal.

Finally, many voice students claim that singing is a type of therapy for them. During vocal therapy, that form of release may be temporarily removed. It is helpful to acknowledge the importance of singing as "therapy" for your student and to help him find an alternative, nonvocal release of stress.

Working with Hoarse Students

Most people have experienced hoarseness at some point in their lives. Usually it is related to a cold, and it goes away within a couple weeks. The hoarseness represents enough of a shift in vocal quality from a person's baseline that others notice the change, but it is caused by illness. This is not the hoarseness to which we are referring here. We are advising vocal trainers to be on the lookout for chronic, perhaps subtle, hoarseness unrelated to upper respiratory illness.

Chronic hoarseness is likely indicative of a voice disorder. It is usually related to laryngeal swelling and tends to first impede clear production of high, soft vocalizations. Students may show a preference for loud vocal production in an effort to overcome hoarseness heard only during soft phonation. If your student has chronic hoarseness, he most likely needs to be referred for a voice evaluation by both an ENT and a voice/speech pathologist. Once a vocalist is evaluated, he may be diagnosed with a vocal fold pathology and referred for voice therapy. Ideally, the voice/speech pathologist and vocal coach or singing teacher will communicate about the students' vocal issues and determine what type of voice work outside of therapy would be appropriate. In general, however, vocal teachers can support their students through continued information on vocal health as well as monitoring of vocal hygiene.

There are some important considerations, which may not be intuitive, for voice coaches and teachers to keep in mind. The first pertains to the limitations of the ear. While the ear is one of the most valuable tools a voice clinician has, it can be misleading. For example, a student who is able to sound good some of the time is not necessarily injury free. Voice coaches have told us that they were not concerned about a student's hoarseness because when the student spoke or sang in a particular way, their voice sounded clear. Particular voice use patterns can make an injured voice sound clear. This is true either because the voice use pattern is therapeutic and is causing (for that moment) healthy vocal fold closure, or because the voice use pattern is causing the student to press the vocal folds into submission. This behavior may create a clear voice in the moment, but exacerbates injury in the long run. Another limitation of the ear relates to diagnosis. Different vocal pathologies can sound the same as each other. A nodule might create a vocal sound that is identical to a cancerous lesion. Trusting our ear as the sole diagnostic tool can be dangerous.

> Remember that the vocal folds do not have pain sensors on them. Therefore, pain is not necessarily an indicator of pathology, and lack thereof does not indicate vocal health.

For teachers working with hoarse students as part of a team (i.e., in academia), there are some additional considerations. If the student is in voice therapy, she may require your assistance. The process of therapy can be like "undressing" the voice, and there may actually be deterioration in vocal quality while the student learns new skills. Voice therapy is not about learning to produce a particular sound, but rather about creating sounds with a particular physiology. Many students acquire their voice disorders by aiming for a certain sound and achieving it in a way that leads to injury. Voice therapy involves removing the compensatory behaviors that a student might be using to make her voice sound better, but that are actually exacerbating the injury. While the voice builds up strength in a healthy way, the sound quality could possibly suffer. You can play an important role by being the student's advocate with other faculty, and explaining that the disruption is both temporary and necessary for healing. Coaches and teachers can also help students navigate any vocal responsibilities they may have ahead of them while preserving their vocal therapy guidelines.

Although we rely on teachers to use their best judgment, a referral for a voice evaluation should be considered in the following cases:

- Vocal hoarseness lasts a week or more without an obvious contributing illness
- Vocal hoarseness associated with illness persists two weeks or more after other symptoms have subsided
- Laryngeal discomfort or voice loss is experienced after strenuous voicing
- Voicing of high pitches at soft volumes is significantly impaired, or becomes less clear over time
- Student reaches a persistent, unexpected plateau in development of vocal range or flexibility

Instrumentation for Voice Analysis

Throughout the country, and the world for that matter, there are many voice clinics designed to evaluate and care for individuals with voice loss or disruption. If at all possible, we recommend that you visit the voice clinic nearest to you before you begin referring your students there. The goal of a voice evaluation is to obtain subjective and (relatively) objective measurements of a patient's voice, then to compare their clinical presentation with normative data. Baseline measurements are also used to track success in restoring voice.

Laryngeal Videostroboscopy

Historically, laryngeal viewing was achieved by placing a laryngeal mirror near the back of the mouth, angling it downward and shining a light on it. The invention of the endoscope revolutionized the way the larynx is viewed. A flexible laryngeal endoscope is about 3.5 mm in diameter and a foot long. Two channels run the length of the endoscope, one to produce light and the other with a lens. It is inserted through the nostril, past the soft palate, and dangled above the larynx. Early versions of the laryngeal endoscope required the physician to look through an eyepiece to see the larynx (imagine looking into a microscope, only the lens of the microscope has been inserted through the nose and down the throat). This procedure is called *laryngeal endoscopy*.

Eventually, the endoscope was coupled to a camera and a monitor allowing for the view to be projected onto a screen. Computer software was developed for capturing views for later analysis. That procedure was called laryngeal *video*endoscopy. Keep in mind that up until this procedure was developed, the view of the larynx had been with the naked eye only. When you consider, however, that human vocal folds can vibrate between 70 and 1,500 times per second, any type of in-depth analysis is seriously restricted by our eyes' inability to track something moving that fast. The solution to this problem was solved initially by flashing a strobe light onto the vocal folds while they were vibrating. Timing the flash to occur at just the right intervals allows the viewer to see the vocal folds in apparent slow motion. This is when "laryngeal videoendoscopy" became "laryngeal video*strobo*scopy" (commonly called a "strobe").

Recent technology, called laryngeal videokymography, records the vibration of the vocal folds under a steady light, and displays the vibration in slow motion. This allows the examiner to see a true representation of each cycle of vocal fold vibration, but the analysis must occur after the examination rather than during, and it can be painstakingly slow. Future technology will most likely involve viewing vocal fold vibration under steady light, yet at a rate that our eyes can handle. Until that technology becomes affordable, easy, and quick to use, the typical voice clinic will have videostroboscopic analysis as its standard of care.

There are two basic types of endoscopes used when examining the larynx. The one we have been discussing is flexible and is snaked through the nose, past the palate, and dangles above the larynx. This one comes in a few different diameters. The benefit of this endoscope is that the patient is able to speak and sing while it is in place, allowing the clinician to evaluate the patient's muscle use patterns. The other basic type of laryngeal endoscope is a rigid rod about one foot long and the diameter of a thick pen. At the tip is an angled lens and a light. This endoscope is inserted through the mouth and the tip hovers above the back of the tongue. It does not go down the throat, but rather peers around the bend of the tongue and visualizes the vocal folds from the back of the mouth. It is also attached to a camera and computer and can use a strobe light. Historically, pictures obtained with this endoscope had better resolution as well as better magnification than the ones obtained via flexible endoscope, because the scope itself is of a larger diameter, so could house a better lens, better magnification, and better fiber optics. With ever-improving technology, the picture quality from the flexible scope now rivals that of the rigid scope.

Laryngeal endoscopy is an essential part of a voice evaluation. Either an otolaryngologist or a speech pathologist will complete the endoscopic evaluation. It will be up to the otolaryngologist to diagnose any laryngeal abnormalities. The speech pathologist will review the endoscopic examination for functional abnormalities. In other words, the speech pathologist will look at the way laryngeal muscles are habitually moving and determine if correction is needed for maladaptive muscle behavior. In some cases, laryngeal endoscopy is used for biofeedback during voice therapy. A well-equipped voice clinic will have at minimum a flexible scope or a rigid endoscope, and all scopes will be stroboscopy compatible.

Acoustic Analysis

A computerized acoustic analysis of voice is another component of a voice evaluation, and is usually completed by a speech-language pathologist. One motivation behind using a computer to analyze a voice is to obtain an "objective" analysis. It should be noted, however, that even our most objective voice measurements still require a good deal of subjective interpretation, and the way in which vocal signals are captured can truly influence the data collected. That being said, the data obtained from a computerized analysis of the voice allows the clinician to establish a well-described, recorded vocal baseline to use for comparison after treatment. This type of analysis also allows the clinician to compare the irregularity of the patient's voice to voices whose qualities fall within normal limits (normative data).

To run a computerized analysis on a voice, the voice must become a digitized signal. The transfer from an acoustic signal to a digital one is completed with a microphone. Every cycle of vocal fold vibration is converted into a complex waveform and can be analyzed and displayed on a screen. A clear voice holding out a steady pitch will generate a digitized vocal signal comprised of a long string of similar complex waveforms. The length, height, and shape of the waveforms are determined by vocal fold vibration. In simple terms, the length of a waveform corresponds with the speed of vocal fold vibration (vocal pitch), and the height of the waveform corresponds with vocal loudness. The shape of the waveform carries information regarding the regularity of vocal fold vibration as well as the harmonic structure and location of formant frequencies. Mathematical algorithms are used to look for regularities in the vocal signal by comparing one waveform with another. When the voice is unclear, neighboring waveforms start to differ, and the degree to which they differ often corresponds with hoarseness severity.

In addition to reporting frequency and intensity of vocal fold vibration and cycle irregularity, a computerized analysis can also generate a spectrogram of the vocal signal. The *spectrogram* is a graph with time on the horizontal axis and frequency on the vertical axis. Intensity, or loudness for our purposes, is displayed as darkness. To construct a spectrogram the fundamental frequency (determined by how many times the vocal folds vibrate each second) as well as the array of overtones are extracted from a digitized vocal signal. Vocal harmonic structure can be viewed and analyzed for noise, regularity of pitch and loudness, formant frequencies, consistency of vocal fold vibration, extent and speed of vibrato for singers, and many other aspects that are helpful when assessing a disorder and planning treatment. The same equipment used for analysis can also be used for biofeedback during voice therapy.

Aerodynamic Analysis

An aerodynamic analysis of voice can also be completed during a voice evaluation, usually by the voice/speech pathologist. This is a nifty way of examining how a patient is passing air through the vocal folds when voicing. The patient is asked to say particular sounds while a soft, plastic mask (similar to an oxygen mask) is held over the mouth and nose and a small tube is inserted just inside the mouth. This mask is equipped with a mechanism that measures the amount of air pressure that is inside the mouth just prior to voicing, as well as the amount of airflow that passes through the mask during voicing. This information is digitized then analyzed, displayed and compared with normative values. From these data, we can gain information about how much air pressure the patient is building up underneath the vocal folds as well as how much airflow he allows during voicing, and we can estimate the vocal fold resistance. We suspect tension when we see high pressure and low airflow. Poor vocal fold contact is suspected if we see high pressure and high airflow. If we see low pressure and low airflow, we may question whether or not the patient is generating enough breath power to speak healthfully. An aerodynamic analysis can also render other data that can further illuminate the path to a good vocal diagnosis. As with endoscopy and computerized acoustic analysis, this equipment can also be used to provide biofeedback to a patient during voice therapy.

The Voice Evaluation

In addition to endoscopic, acoustic, and aerodynamic analyses of the voice, a voice patient undergoing an evaluation can expect an interview as well as questionnaires to obtain a full medical history, a complete profile of symptoms, and to establish any decline of life quality caused by vocal disruption. Finally, a patient's speaking and, when appropriate, singing voice technique is analyzed by the voice/speech pathologist for aberrant alignment, suspected tension, use of resonance, and integration of adequate respiratory support for voicing. The structures involved in speaking are examined for both structural and functional abnormalities. The subjective information is consolidated to formulate a diagnosis as well as a treatment plan which may or may not include medications, voice therapy, or laryngeal surgery.

A well-equipped, well-staffed voice clinic is an excellent resource for you to use when your students present with chronic hoarseness, laryngeal discomfort, or difficulty accessing vocal range and flexibility. "Well-equipped" means that the clinic uses videostroboscopy, acoustic analysis, and aerodynamic analysis. "Well-staffed" means that there is an otolaryngologist, a speech pathologist specializing in voice, and a singing voice specialist in house, plus a referral base for gastroenterologists, psychologists, pulmonologists, and allergists who are sensitive to the needs of a professional vocalist or vocal student. When you are visiting your local voice clinic, be sure to inquire about the equipment used and the experience of the staff.

While going to a voice center is usually ideal, it is not necessarily the only way to receive good care. Some otolaryngologists refer their patients to voice pathologists in a practice other than their own. In these cases, the voice pathologist may be able to obtain adequate information using a laptop computer and a sound level meter.

For a listing of voice clinics in your area, you may want to contact the American Speech-Language and Hearing Association, the Voice Foundation, or the national voice center referral database. Consult the appendix for Web addresses.

Appendix: Organizations and Web Sites

Accent Help
www.accenthelp.com
Offers downloadable audio and written materials for clear speech, accent modification, and dialect acquisition.

American Academy of Otolaryngology—Head and Neck Surgery
www.entnet.org
"Your source for information on the ears, nose, throat, and related structures of the head and neck." Find a voice doctor in your area by using the "Find an ENT" search on the home page and searching for the specialty "laryngology."

American Society for the Alexander Technique
www.alexandertech.org
One of many sites describing the Alexander Technique and offering links to teachers in different areas. A gentle technique to help with optimal muscle use.

American Speech-Language-Hearing Association
www.asha.org
Find a voice therapist near you.

ChatterVox

www.chattervox.com

An example of a self-contained voice amplification system.

Estill Voice Training

www.trainmyvoice.com

Learn about the Estill voice training system, and find a teacher or workshop.

The Feldenkrais Educational Foundation of North America

www.feldenkrais.com

Find a practitioner near you. Body work "for anyone who wants to reconnect with their natural abilities to move, think, and feel."

General American Accent

www.generalamericanaccent.com

Offers downloadable written and audio material for self-study of clear speech in a neutral American dialect.

Love Your Voice!

www.loveyourvoice.com

The authors' Web site. Discover more about our one-day seminar and educational DVDs.

National Association of Teachers of Singing

www.nats.org

Find a singing teacher, or learn how to join if you are a singing teacher.

National Center for Voice & Speech

www.ncvs.org
Resource for information about vocal anatomy, physiology, and health. Includes list of medications and their effects on voice.

National Voice Center Referral Database

www.gbmc.org/voice/national.cfm
Find a voice center in your area.

SoniVox

www.griffinlab.com
An example of a self-contained voice amplification system.

Voice and Speech Trainers Association

www.vasta.org
A service and advocacy organization for voice and speech professionals. Professional index, annual conferences/workshops, professional guidelines, online bibliography and webliography.

Glossary

ALS: Amyotrophic lateral sclerosis, also known as Lou Gehrig's disease, a neurological condition causing progressive deterioration of voluntary muscle function.

Acid reflux: See *GERD* and *LPR*.

Acoustics: The study of sound. For a related meaning, see *room acoustics*.

Air sacs: Informal term for *pulmonary alveoli* referring to small hallow cavities in the lungs that fill with air and allow for oxygenation of blood.

Alexander Technique: A method to aid awareness and change of harmful habits related to physical movement and tension.

Alignment: Relationship of the head to the rest of the body.

Articulators: Parts of the body used to produce speech including the hard palate, soft palate, tongue, teeth, glottis, lower jaw lips, and gum ridge.

Arytenoid cartilages: Two small pyramidal cartilages in the larynx; the back of each vocal fold attaches to an arytenoid.

Autonomic nervous system: The part of the peripheral nervous system responsible for involuntary bodily function.

Bernoulli Effect: A mathematical principle stating the higher the velocity of a fluid, the lower the pressure. The principle explains how air passing between the vocal cords not only blows them apart, but also sucks them back together.

Botox: Botulinum toxin, a neurotoxic protein, injected in small doses into the human body to temporarily paralyze specific muscles. While known as a cosmetic injection, it is also used to treat spasmodic dysphonia.

Cartilage: Dense connective tissue found throughout the body that is softer and more malleable than bone.

Chakra: Sanskrit word meaning *wheel*. Refers to energy centers in the body, commonly located at a nerve plexus.

Consonant cluster: Two or more consonants in a row.

Cricoarytenoid muscles: Muscles running from the cricoid cartilage to the arytenoid cartilage. The posterior branch contributes to bringing together the two arytenoids and vocal folds, and the lateral branch pulls the arytenoids and vocal folds apart from each other.

Cricoid cartilage: The second largest cartilage in the larynx.

Cricothyroid muscle: Muscles running from the cricoid cartilage to the thyroid cartilage, responsible for pitch elevation through vocal fold elongation.

Diaphragm: A dome-shaped sheet of muscle at the bottom of the rib cage that, when contracted, flattens out and thereby enlarges the thoracic cavity. Primary muscle of inhalation.

Diction: The way in which words are pronounced.

Easy onset: Beginning words that start with a vowel sound in such a way that the sound is smooth rather than harsh or choppy.

ENT: Ear, nose, and throat physician. See *otolaryngologist.*

Epiglottis: Leaf-shaped cartilage in the larynx that covers the entrance to the airway during swallowing.

Epithelium: A thin tissue that lines cavities and structures of the body, including the vocal folds.

Esophagus: A muscular tube through which food passes from the throat to the stomach.

Essential tremor: Neurological condition involving tremor of the head, hands, voice, arms, or other body part, not caused by other diseases or conditions.

False vocal cords: See *ventricular folds.*

Feldenkrais Method: A method to improve physical movement and function.

Floating ribs: The 11th and 12th paired ribs that, unlike ribs 1 through 10, have only one attachment (to the vertebrae).

Formant: Peaks in the frequency spectrum caused by resonance of the vocal tract. Vowels are identified based on different formants.

Forward focus: Using the voice in such a way that it feels placed at the front of the mouth or face. Produces a lot of sound for little stress on the system. Also known as forward placement.

Forward resonance: Feeling vibrations in facial bones during phonation.

Frequency: Rate of vibration (of the vocal folds).

Fundamental frequency: The frequency in a tone with the most energy and the one we identify as the tone's pitch. In voice, the number of times per second the vocal folds vibrate.

Gastroenterologist: A medical doctor specializing in issues of the digestive system.

GERD: Gastroesophageal reflux disease. The regurgitation of stomach juices, including acid, into the esophagus.

Glottal attack: Closing of the vocal folds, and usually the false vocal folds, followed by a sudden release; creates a sound like that in the middle of the word "uh-oh."

Gum ridge: For the purpose of this book, the term is used to refer to portion of the hard palate just above the upper teeth. Also called the *alveolar arch*.

Harmonics: See *overtones*.

Hertz: Cycles per second, abbreviated Hz. Used to measure rate of vibration. The vocal folds vibrate at about 100 to 200 Hz during speech for most adults.

Hyoid bone: The only bone in the larynx. Supports muscles for speech and swallowing. Also the only bone in the body that does not articulate with another bone.

Intensity: Here used as synonymous with *sound intensity*, referring to the amount of energy in a sound wave. Perceived as loudness and measured in decibels (dB).

Interarytenoid muscles: Muscles between the arytenoid cartilages that when contracted assist in bringing together the two arytenoids as well as the vocal folds.

Intercostal muscles: Muscles between the ribs that cause the rib cage to expand and contract during breathing.

Lactic acid: A substance that builds up in an overused muscle, resulting in an acidic environment that interferes with the muscle's ability to use energy.

Laryngeal endoscopy: A technique for visualizing the larynx via a small tube inserted through the nose or mouth.

Laryngologist: An otolaryngologist specializing in diagnosis and treatment of the voice and larynx.

Larynx: The cartilaginous structure that houses the vocal folds. Also known as voice box and Adam's apple.

Ligament: Dense, fibrous, elastic tissue connecting two bony structures in the body.

Linking: Connecting words together so there is a feeling of flow to speech.

Lip trills: Rolling the lips with breath, making a sound like a motorboat. Generates healthy movement of the vocal cords and helps to warm up the voice.

LPR: Laryngopharyngeal reflux. Acid reflux involving stomach juices coming up the esophagus, out the upper esophageal sphincter, and onto the vocal cords. Heartburn may not be a symptom; can cause voice problems.

Masseter: The main muscle responsible for closing the jaw and biting.

Maxilla: The upper jaw bone, located under and next to the nose. Upper teeth insert into it, and it connects to the cheekbones.

Myasthenia gravis: A chronic autoimmune neuromuscular disease resulting in muscle weakness, usually more severe with use and better with rest.

Nasal cavity: Space behind your nose and above the roof of your mouth.

Nasal resonance: Sound created when the soft palate is dropped during phonation and sound energy is allowed to pass through the nose. The only sounds in English created with nasal resonance are *m*, *n*, and *ng*.

Optimal speech breathing: Providing adequate airflow for speech production while minimizing tension and effort.

Optimum vocal efficiency: Vocal fold vibration that results in strong sound quality achieved with minimum wear and tear on the body.

Otolaryngologist: A medical doctor specializing in the ear, nose, and throat. Subspecialties also exist within these arenas. See also *laryngologist*.

Overtones: Vibrations or resonances of a system. In voice production, they are multiples of the fundamental frequency. Also known as harmonics and partials.

Paradoxical breathing: The act of inflating the chest and contracting the abdominal muscles during inhalation instead of allowing the belly to expand.

Paradoxical vocal fold movement: Closure of the vocal folds when they would normally be open, such as during respiration. Because it causes difficulty with breathing, it can be mistaken for asthma.

Parkinson disease: A neurological condition causing tremor, stiffness, slowness of movement, and impaired balance.

Pharynx: A tube of muscles running from the nose and back of the mouth down to the larynx.

Phonation: The act of making sound with the vocal cords.

Phonatory system: Referring to the structure and function of the larynx, or voice box.

Pitch: The perception of how high or low a sound is. Generally determined by frequency (speed) of vibration, with a higher frequency yielding a higher pitch.

Plosive: A consonant created by temporarily halting airflow by occluding the vocal tract with the articulators, then releasing the air.

Professional voice user: Anyone who relies on his voice to fulfill his job requirements. Examples are managers, lawyers, clergy, coaches, teachers, singers, politicians, and actors.

Recurrent laryngeal nerve: A branch of the vagus cranial nerve that supplies energy to the larynx. Damage can result in vocal cord paralysis.

Reinforcement: Amplification, enhancement.

Resonant frequency: The frequency at which an object or tube vibrates most strongly.

Resonatory system: Referring here to the upper respiratory tract (larynx, pharynx, nose, and mouth) through which sound is propagated and modified for speech.

Respiratory system: Referring here to the lower respiratory tract (the trachea, bronchi, and lungs) and the surrounding bones, cartilage, muscles, and tissue involved in the exchange of gases required for life.

Room acoustics: Modification of sound due to room dimensions, surfaces, and contents.

Selective amplification: A tube's ability to enhance certain aspects of a sound based on its own shape and size.

Singer's formant: An amplification of energy at around 3,000 Hz that causes a singer's voice to "ring" and project over the sounds of an orchestra.

Soft palate: The soft, back-most part of the roof of the mouth. Made of muscle and other tissue, the soft palate can drop, thereby opening a passageway into the nasal cavity, or it can elevate and separate the nasal cavity from the mouth.

Spasmodic dysphonia: A neurological condition causing the vocal cords to spasm open or closed during speech.

Spectrogram: A graph displaying intensity (loudness) and frequency (pitch and harmonics) over time used to analyze voice.

Speech: Decodable sounds that carry meaning created through a series of complex movements involving the tongue, lips, soft palate, hard palate, lower jaw, teeth, gum ridge, vocal folds, and lungs.

Stage fright: Extreme discomfort experienced when speaking, singing, or otherwise performing for others. Discomfort can occur during or before the required public act. Symptoms can include but are not limited to pounding heart, shaking, intestinal pain, dry mouth, and profuse sweating.

Stylohyoid ligament: A ligament running from the hyoid bone in the larynx to the styloid process in the skull.

Styloid process: Part of the temporal bone anchoring several muscles of the larynx and tongue.

Swing thought: A mental exercise in the game of golf wherein a single thought is held in one's mind while swinging the club.

Temporomandibular joint: The structure of the jaw joining the temporal bone and the masseter that enables opening and closing of the mouth.

Thoracic cavity: A chamber in the human body created by the rib cage, spine, and diaphragm containing the lungs, trachea, bronchi, esophagus, and heart with associated nerves, vessels, lymphatic tissue, and glands.

Thorax: The region of the human body extending from the neck to the diaphragm.

Thyroarytenoid muscles: The muscles of the vocal folds, which contribute to vocal fold shortening, vibration, and closure.

Thyroid cartilage: The largest cartilage in the larynx, to which the front of each vocal fold is attached.

Torso: The central part of the human body from which neck and limbs extend.

Trachea: The airway, beginning at the larynx and extending down into the lungs. Also known as the windpipe.

Tuvan singers: Throat singers from Tuva who use harmonics to create two sounds at the same time.

Uvula: Part of the soft palate that dangles at the back of the throat.

Ventricular folds: Also known as false vocal folds. Primarily comprised of mucous membrane, glands, and muscle fibers extending from the vocal folds. Not typically used in voice production, they protect the airway during swallowing.

Vertebra: One of 33 bones that make up the human spine.

Videolaryngostroboscopy: A method of visualizing the vocal folds using a computerized camera and a flashing light. Allows for magnification of the vocal folds as well as the illusion of slow motion vibration for diagnostic purposes. Also known as videostroboscopy, stroboscopy, and strobe. See also *laryngeal endoscopy.*

Vocal fatigue: A sensation of tiredness or aching around the larynx. Can result in effortful speech.

Vocal fold nodule: Mass lesion on the vocal fold, similar to a callous, caused in part by vocal use. Typically arises at the middle point of the vibrating vocal fold edge on both vocal folds. Less frequently, can occur on only one vocal fold. Also known as nodes.

Vocal fold paresis: Weakness of the vocal cord caused by nerve or muscle damage.

Vocal fold polyp: Mass lesion on the vocal cords, similar to a blister, usually caused in part by voice use.

Vocal folds: Two bands of muscle covered by specialized tissue that valve the breath and vibrate to create voice. Their primary biological function, however, is to protect the airway. Also known as vocal cords; sometimes called the *true* vocal folds to distinguish them from the *false* vocal folds that are located above them.

Vocal image: An impression of personal character conveyed through vocal tone quality.

Vocal injury: A disruption of vocal fold vibration due to disadvantageous changes of the vocal fold tissue or laryngeal muscles.

Vocal mechanism: The structure and function of the larynx.

Vocal placement: A perception that sound energy created from vocal fold vibration is concentrated and felt in the head, face, or chest.

Vocal tract: The cavity running from the larynx to the lips, and also including the nose; acts as a filter for sound.

Voice: Sound resulting from vocal fold vibration.

Voiceprint: Everything that makes a person's individual voice unique.

Voiced consonant: A nonvowel speech sound produced with vocal fold vibration, e.g., *b*, *d*, *v*.

Voiceless consonant: A nonvowel speech sound produced without vocal fold vibration, e.g., *p*, *t*, *s*.

Waveform: In the context of voice production, the shape of a plot of changes in air pressure resulting from vocal fold vibration quantified against atmospheric air pressure and tracked over time.

References

Berry, Cicely. *Voice and the Actor*. New York: Collier Books, 1973.

Berry, David A., Katherine Verdolini, Douglas W. Montequin, Markus M. Hess, Roger W. Chan, and Ingo R. Titze. "A Quantitative Output-Cost Ratio in Voice Production." *Journal of Speech, Language, and Hearing Research* 44 (February 2001): 29–37.

Bloom, Barbara, and Robin A. Cohen. "Summary Health Statistics for U.S. Children: National Health Interview Survey, 2006." *Vital and Health Statistics* 10, no. 234 (2007).

Brennan, Barbara. *Hands of Light*. New York: Bantam Books, 1987.

Cameron, Julia. *The Artist's Way*. New York: Jeremy P. Tarcher/Putnam, 1992.

Catten, Michael, Steven D. Gray, Thomas H. Hammond, Ruixia Zhou, and Elizabeth H. Hammond. "Analysis of Cellular Location and Concentration in Vocal Fold Lamina Propria." *Otolaryngology—Head & Neck Surgery* 118, no. 5 (May 1998): 663–637.

Cohen, Jacob T., Kevin K. Bach, Gregory N. Postma, and James A. Koufman. "Clinical Manifestations of Laryngopharyngeal Reflux." *Ear, Nose & Throat Journal* 81, no. 9, suppl. no. 2 (September 2002): 19–23.

Cookman, Starr, and Katherine Verdolini. "Interrelation of Mandibular and Laryngeal Functions." *Journal of Voice* 13, no. 1 (March 1999): 11–24.

Cooper, Donald S., and Ingo R. Titze. "Generation and Dissipation of Heat in Vocal Fold Tissue." *Journal of Speech and Hearing Research* 28, no. 2 (June 1985): 207–215.

DelGaudio, John M. "Steroid Inhaler Laryngitis: Dysphonia Caused by Inhaled Fluticasone Therapy." *Archives of Otolaryngology Head-Neck Surgery* 128, no. 6 (June 2002): 677–681.

DeVore, Kate. "To Refer or Not to Refer." In *The Voice and Speech Review: The Voice in Violence.* Cincinnati, OH: VASTA, 2001.

———. "Voice Care Tips for Clinicians." *ADVANCE for Speech-Language Pathologists* 14, no. 3 (January 19, 2004): 9.

DeVore, Kate, and Katherine Verdolini. "Professional Speaking Voice Training and Applications to Speech-Language Pathology." *Current Opinion in Otolaryngology & Head and Neck Surgery* 6 (1998): 145–150.

Estill, Jo. *Primer of Compulsory Figures.* Santa Rosa, CA: Estill Voice Training Systems, 2003.

Farhi, Donna. *The Breathing Book: Vitality and Good Health through Essential Breath Work.* New York: Holt and Company, 1996.

Gardner, Joy. *Pocket Guide to Chakras.* Freedom, CA: The Crossing Press, 1998.

———. *The Healing Voice.* Freedom, CA: The Crossing Press, 1993.

Glickstein, Lee. *Be Heard Now!* New York: Broadway Books, 1998.

Gray, Steven D., Ingo R. Titze, Fariborz Alipour, and Thomas H. Hammond. "Biomechanical and Histological Observations of Vocal Fold Fibrous Proteins." *Annals of Otology, Rhinology & Laryngology* 109, no. 1 (January 2000): 77–85.

Hampton, Marion, and Barbara Acker, eds. *The Vocal Vision: Views on Voice.* New York: Applause, 1997.

Hay, Louise. *You Can Heal Your Life.* Carson, CA: Hay House, 1984.

Jiang, Jack. J., Carlos E. Diaz, and David G. Hanson. "Finite Element Modeling of Vocal Fold Vibration in Normal Phonation and Hyperfunctional Dysphonia: Implications for the Pathogenesis of Vocal Nodules." *Annals of Otology, Rhinology & Laryngology* 107, no. 7 (July 1998): 603–610.

Jiang, Jack. J., Anand G. Shah, Markus M. Hess, Katherine Verdolini, Franklin M. Banzali, and David G. Hanson. "Vocal Fold Impact Stress Analysis." *Journal of Voice* 15, no. 1 (March 2001): 4–14.

Jiang, Jack J., and Ingo R. Titze. "Measurement of Vocal Fold Intraglottal Pressure and Impact Stress." *Journal of Voice* 8, no. 2 (June 1994): 132–144.

Koufman, Jamie A. "Laryngopharyngeal Reflux Is Different From Classic Gastroesophageal Reflux Disease." *Ear, Nose & Throat Journal* 81, no. 9, suppl. no. 2 (September 2002): 7–9.

Koufman, James A., Milan R. Amin, and Marguerite Panetti. "Prevalence of Reflux in 113 Consecutive Patients with Laryngeal and Voice Disorders." *Otolaryngololgy—Head & Neck Surgery* 123, no. 4 (October 2000): 385–388.

Koufman, Jamie A., Gregory A. Postma, Michelle M. Cummins, and P. David Blalock. "Vocal Fold Paresis." *Otolaryngololgy—Head & Neck Surgery* 122, no. 4 (April 2000): 537–541.

Lavy, J. A., G. Wood, J. S. Rubin, and M. Harries. "Dysphonia Associated with Inhaled Steroids." *Journal of Voice* 14, no. 4 (December 2000): 581–588.

Lessac, Arthur. *The Use and Training of the Human Voice: A Bio-dynamic Approach to Vocal Life, Third Edition.* Mountain View, CA: Mayfield Publishing Company, 1997.

———. *The Use and Training of the Human Voice: A Practical Approach to Speech and Voice Dynamics.* New York: DBS Publications, 1967.

Lindblom, Bjorn E., and Johann E. Sundberg. "Acoustical Consequences of Lip, Tongue, Jaw, and Larynx Movement." *Journal of the Acoustical Society of America* 50, no. 4 (May 1971): 1,166–1,179.

Linklater, Kristin. *Freeing the Natural Voice*. New York: Drama Book Publishers, 1976.

Miller, Marcie K., and Katherine Verdolini. "Frequency and Risk Factors for Voice Problems in Teachers of Singing and Control Subjects." *Journal of Voice* 9, no. 4 (December 1995): 348–362.

Mirza, Natasha, Sandra Kasper Schwartz, and Danielle Antin-Ozerkis. "Laryngeal Findings in Users of Combination Corticosteroid and Bronchodilator Therapy." *Laryngoscope* 114, no. 9 (September 2004): 1,566–1,569.

Modisett, Noah, and James Luter. *Speaking Clearly*. 5th ed. Boston: Pearson Custom Publishing, 2006.

Neutral American Speech. Accent Help, www.accenthelp.com (accessed May 31, 2008).

Peterson K. L., Katherine Verdolini-Marston, Julie M. Barkmeier, and Harry T. Hoffman. "Comparison of Aerodynamic and Electroglottographic Parameters in Evaluating Clinically Relevant Voicing Patterns." *Annals of Otology, Rhinology & Laryngology* 103 (1994): 335–346.

Pleis, John R., and Margaret Lethbridge-Cejku. "Summary Health Statistics for U.S. Adults: National Health Interview Survey, 2005." *Vital and Health Statistics* 10, no. 232 (2006).

Pond, David. *Chakras for Beginners*. St. Paul, MN: Llewellyn Publications, 2000.

Raphael, Bonnie N. "A Consumer's Guide to Voice and Speech Training." In *The Vocal Vision: Views on Voice*, ed. by M. Hampton and B. Acker. New York: Applause, 1997.

Raphael, Bonnie N., and Robert T. Sataloff. "Increasing Vocal Effectiveness." In *Professional Voice: The Science and Art of Clinical Care*, 2nd ed., ed. by R. T. Sataloff. San Diego: Plural Publishing, 1997, 721–729.

Richter, Bernhard, Erwin Lohle, Bettina Knapp, Matthias Weikert, Josef Schlomicher-Their, and Katherine Verdolini. "Harmful Substances on the Opera Stage: Possible Negative Effects on Singers' Respiratory Tracts." *Journal of Voice* 16, no. 1 (March 2002): 72–80.

Rodenburg, Patsy. *The Right to Speak*. New York: Routledge, 1992.

Rodgers, Janet, ed. *The Complete Voice and Speech Workout*. New York: Applause, 2002.

Schneider, Carol M., Keith G. Saxon, and Carolyn A. Dennehy. "Exercise Physiology: Perspective for Vocal Training." In *Professional Voice: The Science and Art of Clinical Care*, 2nd ed., ed. by R. T. Sataloff. San Diego: Plural Publishing, 1997, 775–779.

Skinner, Edith. *Speak with Distinction*. New York: Applause, 1990.

Story, Brad H., Ingo R. Titze, and Eric A. Hoffman. "The Relationship of Vocal Tract Shape to Three Voice Qualities." *Journal of the Acoustical Society of America* 109, no. 4 (April 2001): 1,651–1,667.

Titze, Ingo R. "Mechanical Stress in Phonation." *Journal of Voice* 8, no. 2 (June 1994): 99–105.

———. *Principles of Voice Production*. Englewood Cliffs, NJ: Prentice-Hall, 1994.

Verdolini, Katherine. "Principles of Skill Acquisition Applied to Voice Training." *NCVS Status and Progress Report* 6 (May 1994): 155–163.

Verdolini, Katherine, David G. Druker, Phyllis M. Palmer, and Hani Samawi. "Laryngeal Adduction in Resonant Voice." *Journal of Voice* 12, no. 3 (September 1998): 315–327.

Verdolini, Katherine, Young Min, Ingo R. Titze, Jon Lemke, Kice Brown, Miriam van Mersbergen, Jack Jiang, and Kim Fisher. "Biological Mechanisms Underlying Voice Changes Due to Dehydration." *Journal of Speech Language and Hearing Research* 45, no. 2 (April 2002): 268–281.

Verdolini, Katherine, and Lorraine O. Ramig. "Review: Occupational Risks for Voice Problems." *Logopedics, Phoniatrics, Vocology* 26, no. 1 (2001): 37–46.

Verdolini, Katherine, and Ingo R. Titze. "The Application of Laboratory Formulas to Clinical Voice Management." *American Journal of Speech-Language Pathology* 4 (1995): 62–69.

Verdolini, Katherine, Ingo R. Titze, and Ann Fennell. "Dependence of Phonatory Effort on Hydration Level." *Journal of Speech & Hearing Research* 37, no. 5 (October 1994): 1,001–1,007.

Verdolini-Marston, Katherine, and D. A. Balota. "The Role of Elaborative and Perceptual-Integrative Processes in Perceptual-Motor Performance." *Journal of Experimental Psychology: Learning, Memory, and Cognition* 20 (1994): 739–749.

Verdolini-Marston, Katherine, Mary K. Burke, Arthur Lessac, Leslie Glaze, and Elizabeth Caldwell. "A Preliminary Study on Two Methods of Treatment for Laryngeal Nodules." *Journal of Voice* 9 (1995): 74–85.

Williams, Alan J., M. S Baghat, D. E. Stableforth, R. M. Cayton, P. M. Shenoi, and Craig Skinner. "Dysphonia Caused by Inhaled Steroids: Recognition of a Characteristic Laryngeal Abnormality." *Thorax* 38 no. 11 (November 1983): 813–821.

Index

The Voice Book Audio CD Track List

1. Introduction
2. Listening Exercise
3. Alignment Exercises
4. Breathing Exercises
5. Resonance Exercises
6. Easy Onset and Linking
7. Emphasis Examples
8. Articulation Exercises
9. Complete Vocal Warm-Up
10. Vocal Cool-Down
11. Gentle Throat Clearing, Delayed Onset, and Speaking Over Background Noise
12. Parting Thoughts

Kate DeVore is a theater voice/speech/dialect trainer, a voice/speech pathologist, and a personal development coach. She operates Total Voice, Inc., (www.TotalVoice.net) in Chicago, where she coaches professional voice users who range from actors to executives. She also teaches at the School at Steppenwolf and Columbia College and lectures nationally and abroad. Kate is the cocreator of downloadable dialect training materials (www.AccentHelp.com) and the author of downloadable material for accent modification (www.GeneralAmericanAccent.com).

Starr Cookman is a clinical voice/speech pathologist, a singing-voice instructor, and an assistant professor in the Division of Otolaryngology at the University of Connecticut School of Medicine. She lectures and teaches workshops on the topic of voice to a variety of audiences. Starr is also a professional mezzo-soprano, specializing in jazz and children's music (www.StarrandShello.com). She lives in Collinsville, Connecticut, with her husband and two children.

Kate and Starr collaborate to present vocal health workshops and created the Laryngeal Teaching Series, instructional DVDs that show endoscopic footage of the throat during speaking, singing, and other forms of sound production (www.LoveYourVoice.com).